# SLEEP TRAINING LIKE A PRO

## A SURVIVAL GUIDE FOR QUALITY SLEEP FOR BABIES, KIDS, AND PARENTS

## ALFIE THOMAS

# CONTENTS

*For Mirabelle, Mercy, Ava and Mia*

## Now I Lay Her Down to Sleep (The Honest Version)

*Now I lay her down to sleep,*
*I beg the Lord, "Eight hours, please!"*
*May angels watch her through the night*
*and keep her eyelids sealed uptight.*
*If she should cry before I wake,*
*just once, Lord, let the monitor break.*

---

*Wishing all my fellow parents eight hours of undis-*
*turbed sleep—tonight and every night . . .*

— BY LIZZY

---

# SLEEP, WHAT'S THAT?

It was the first Saturday night out for Mirabelle and me with our friends. We were excited and giddy like two teenagers given permission to stay out late. (Yes, that's exactly what parenthood feels like when you get time for yourself.) We had put our four-month-old Mercy to sleep, and Mirabelle's mother had volunteered to babysit for the night.

Mirabelle and I were ready to step out and paint the town red! Just then, we heard a soft knock on our door. It was Mirabelle's mother with news that Mercy was up and crying. We weren't about to let this hinder our plans. After all, we were parents now, and we were prepared for whatever life threw at us; we could handle it. Armed with determination, Mirabelle went to Mercy's nursery to put her back to sleep while I waited in the living room, playing games on my mobile phone to kill time. I remember checking the time, it was 8:07 p.m..

After that, everything blurred and seemed like a faded memory. I remember waking with a jolt and checking my watch—10:15 p.m. I panicked and checked my phone only to see at least 10 missed calls from our friends. I rushed to the nursery and there Mirabelle was, seated in her armchair, feet resting on the foot stool, fast asleep with Mercy in her arms. The next day, Mirabelle and I had a good laugh about it, while our friends sympathized with us.

If that doesn't illustrate exactly what parenthood is like, then I don't know what will. Our sleep patterns were all over the place after Mercy's birth. We would find ourselves snoozing in all the corners of the house. We would be up at night trying to put Mercy to sleep and then spend our days catching sleep every time we put her down to nap. Sleep (or sleep deprivation) was the theme of our life when Mercy was born. To say it was difficult to manage—with sleep deprivation, irritability, responsibilities, and jobs—would be an understatement; however, we learned as we went along. We made our fair share of mistakes and bloopers, we laughed, cried, and smiled. There were days when we would be extremely harsh with ourselves and each other, and there were days when we thought, *Yes, we have finally nailed it, and everything will be amazing from now on.*

As Eddie Redmayne said on *The Ellen DeGeneres Show*, when asked about sleep after having a baby, "... suddenly you're the guy who's floating in a constant jetlag with an I.V. of caffeine. And so, I've become that person. But it's worth it." This describes the first few years of parenting perfectly. And it's not just Redmayne who feels it. I can guarantee that nearly every parent feels this way with their first newborn baby. Rather than just listening and agreeing with Redmayne's statement, I decided to make an active change in my sleep patterns when we had our second and third child. I consider myself a professional in the world of sleep now.

Each child gifted us with more experience and strategies to combat the sleeplessness. When Ava, our second child, was born, Mirabelle and I had learned lessons and understood how to navigate our way through parenthood better. When our third child, Mia, was born, we were armed and ready for sleep training. This preparation made our second and third times much easier than the days we spent struggling with Mercy.

I will be sharing these tips in this book to ensure other parents do not pay the price that I already did. I am sharing at least 10 years' worth of experience with you.

I know what you are experiencing, and I want to tell you that it will be okay.

If you are a new parent, or on to your second or third child and feel constantly sleep deprived, restless, scattered, and frustrated, I assure you, you are not alone. You may think or may have heard that newborn babies usually start sleeping by the fourth or fifth month. While this is sometimes true and you will get better sleep eventually, it is not always the case. You may feel confused and lost. You may have a child with special needs who will require more attention. You may have tried different sleep training methods, but they were too general or were not suitable for your family setup.

Nearly every parent around the world feels and experiences what you are feeling.

Parenting may not be easy to begin with, but it takes time, so have patience with yourself and trust the process. As the famous Bantu saying goes, "Patience is the mother of a beautiful child." I sincerely hope you are still awake and alert enough to read what this book will equip you with by the time you are done completing it. You may think sleep is a natural component of our biology and you will just wing it, but believe me, it is better to be informed, equipped with knowledge, and aware rather than just playing the guessing game.

By the end of this book, you will have accomplished the following:

- Learn how being a new parent affects sleep patterns and the factors that may cause sleep deprivation.
- Understand how sleep cycles work for both adults and children at different ages.
- Know how to sleep coach children up to 8 years divided into these sections:

  ○ Newborns and infants
  ○ Toddlers
  ○ Preschoolers
  ○ School-going kids

- Discover important and detrimental bedtime habits.
- Know the five popular sleep training techniques and how to use them.
- Find out how to sleep train special needs children and multiples.
- Discover common sleep disorders among kids.
- Know how to be consistent in their sleep training routine.

Having experienced both sleep deprivation and the lack of it, I am eager to share my knowledge with other parents. I believe that well-rested parents and children are happiest, and I seek to help you to experience better sleep patterns which leads to a better quality of life for the whole family.

# 1

# LITTLE LIGHT SLEEPERS

B efore Mirabelle and I had Mercy, our house was known as the party house. We always had friends and family over, and we did not have children, while our other friends and relatives did. We didn't think twice before having guests over until after 10p.m., returning home late at night, or hosting drinks and games. Everything took a drastic turn when Mercy was born. And this drastic turn took us to new places we had very little clue as to how to navigate.

If someone had asked Mirabelle and I to host a dinner or drinks in the first year after Mercy entering our lives, we would have looked at them and laughed. During the first few days of Mercy coming home, Mirabelle and I were overwhelmed, anxious, and sleep deprived. After all, we had a tiny human to look after.

Since I had done extensive reading, watched videos, and spoken to parents, I had a fair idea of how our situation would change. However, actually living it is an entirely new learning experience. Thankfully, when Ava and Mia were born, Mirabelle and I were more prepared, adept, and flexible thanks to the lessons we learned with Mercy. Practice does make one perfect!

One of the most important pieces of advice that stuck with me was how parents' sleep patterns need to be in sync with their newborn baby's sleep patterns. Luckily, everyone ends up adjusting, and that kept me going. My workplace was extremely accommodating when Mercy was born. I was given two months of paternity leave, and I was able to help Mirabelle and spend time with our child. Most parents hear the word "office leave" and automatically think it means sleeping, socializing, and downtime. Mine was the opposite. During those two months, a good night's sleep was the last thing I got. There were times when I would find myself daydreaming about sleeping for eight hours straight, without any interruptions.

## NEW PARENT, NEW PATTERNS OF SLEEP

Your sleeping patterns will change once you enter the realm of parenthood. There may be nights when you will be restless, anticipating your baby crying. You may not be able to sleep because you must feed your baby every two to three hours, or you may have a hard time falling back asleep after any interruptions. On an average, while men lose around 13 minutes of sleep per night, it is the mothers who lose the most sleep—over an hour each night.

New parents can potentially lose around 600 hours of sleep during their baby's first year. Moreover, your sleeping patterns will not return to pre-pregnancy levels until your child is at least six years old. But it does happen, so do not lose hope.

It comes as no surprise that new mothers and fathers are also at a high risk of insomnia, anxiety, fatigue, depression, and daytime sleepiness. Moreover, these issues become are even more dangerous for mothers experiencing postpartum depression, since sleep deprivation is known to worsen it. A marked decrease in reproductive hormones, which affects the body clock, also adds to a change in sleeping patterns. Even fathers suffer from postpartum depression after the birth of their baby. During all three pregnancies, I used to feel a lot of guilt thinking about how Mirabelle was the one who was healing from pregnancy and childbirth, breastfeeding our children, and being present around the clock. I communicated this to her and did the best I could in terms of supporting her in every way possible.

While it is imperative that your child should sleep well, it is also important to give yourself enough sleep because you are the caregiver and need to be in a healthy and functioning space of mind to give the best care to your baby. Remember to pay attention to your needs as well. Granted, your life might be hectic, but you must make yourself a priority.

What should you expect when you return from the hospital during the first three months? Well, put simply, every baby is unique and will have different patterns, but you can expect not to get a lot of sleep. Newborn babies sleeping habits are very unpredictable. It will be daunting as well, but you will get through it.

BREASTFEEDING AND SLEEP

When you become a parent, one decision that will affect your sleep patterns is whether you will breastfeed your baby or feed them formula. Parents who opt to breastfeed might observe notable changes to their sleep patterns. Studies suggest that babies who are breastfed show more awakenings as opposed to babies who are given formula. Moreover, breastfed babies tend to wake up more easily than formula fed babies. Therefore, breastfeeding mothers will naturally wake up more frequently through the night.

As you read earlier, new parents can fall asleep anywhere and anytime of the day. While this may be comical at times, it could also pose a hazard if you are alone with your baby. If you opt to breastfeed your baby find the safest place where you know you will not fall asleep while breastfeeding. Choose places without any hazards for you and your baby. For instance, look out for sheets, blankets, and edges with no safety boundaries for the baby. If you do end up falling asleep while breastfeeding, which may happen at times, just remember to put your baby back in their original sleeping place to keep the pattern intact.

SLEEP

There are some people who can function on minimum sleep, and you will hear them say, "Sleep is a waste of time." (I am not one of them.) Then there are some people who need a nap during the day to recharge and still others who cannot function without a good night's sleep.

Sleep is vital to keep our brains functioning. On average, an adult needs between seven and nine hours of sleep each night (*Cdc - How Much Sleep Do I Need?*, 2019).

As we fall asleep, our brain's electrical activity changes. Alpha brain waves give way to the large, slow theta and delta waves. When we enter Rapid Eye Movement sleep (REM), our brain is just as active as when we are awake. When we fall asleep, our brain sorts through the memories of the day and strengthens the important ones in a process called consolidation. Scientists think the brain does that by replaying memories. When a new memory is formed, your neurons fire in a specific pattern, and when you sleep, your brain replays those patterns. If you can remember a gift you got on your fifth birthday, thank the restful nights that followed.

A good night's sleep has immediate benefits as well. Lack of sleep can make you feel sluggish, forgetful, and distracted. Longer periods of sleep deprivation can make you more irritable, angry, and stressed out. That is because poor sleep impairs communication within the parts of the brain that deal with planning and self-control. The prefrontal cortex and the amygdala work together to keep your emotions in check. When they are out of sorts, so are you! Since you know how vital good sleep is, you now know that you must not deprive yourself of it. As a new parent, however, sleep patterns and habits will be affected and will change—possibly suffer.

Sleep deprivation can make you do the strangest and funniest things. Mirabelle and I had our fair share of experiences. One of my more amusing memories is the day I had returned home from work and was standing at my front door while pressing the unlock button on my key fob. I grew impatient, pressing the button harder and harder. When all of the sudden, I realized I was trying to open my front door with my car keys. I had to stand there and laugh at myself for a few seconds before going inside.

When we had our first child and I returned to work, Mirabelle was home alone with Mercy. It was not entirely easy for her to manage. Once, during the middle of the workday, I received a call from her, and she could not stop laughing. Turns out, when she took a quick shower after putting Mercy to sleep, she had forgotten to take her bra off and showered with it on.

We were not alone in our sleep deprivations. Mirabelle's sister, for example, shared with us one of her own stories. One morning she had woken up feeling disoriented, and when she glanced towards her baby sleeping in the crib, she noticed a stain underneath her. It was then that she remembered waking up in the middle of the night to change her daughter's diaper, without putting on a new, clean one.

SLEEP DEPRIVATION

Sleep deprivation is a very real thing. With night-time feeding, anxiety, and stress, this can take a toll on sleeping habits and patterns. You will see a distinct change in your moods. Sleep deprivation can cause the following:

- **Irritability:** Do you remember the time you did not get a good night's sleep before going to work the next day? How irritable, unfocused, and edgy were you? Well, apply the same feelings to when you wake up every day on minimum sleep to tend to your baby.
- **Anxiety and Depression:** Due to lack of enough sleep, new parents are at a higher risk for experiencing severe mood swings, anxiety, and depression. If you find yourself experiencing this more than usual, please contact a healthcare provider or speak to your therapist.
- **Accidents and Injuries:** Without a good night's sleep, you are at a higher risk of accidents. This is because sleep deprivation can cause delayed reaction times. Do not drive or operate machinery when you are sleep deprived. (Good

sleep is not subjective; good sleep constitutes seven to nine hours.)

### Sleep Deprivation and Postpartum Depression

What is postpartum depression? It refers to women (and men) suffering from depression post birth. It is more common than you might think. It affects 15 to 20% of mothers. Sometimes new mothers question whether they have postpartum depression because they compare their own feelings to symptoms they have come across in the media. As a husband, I was more mindful of being available, patient, and compassionate towards Mirabelle during her post pregnancy. As a father, I tried to be there as much as I could for my daughters without asking Mirabelle for help in places I could manage on my own. Being there for your partner during this phase is crucial. If you are a husband and your wife is going through postpartum depression, remember to speak to her and hear her out. Help her wherever you think you can. Ask her if she needs help and be patient and kind!

The most common symptoms of postpartum depression include the following:

- You feel sad and tearful.
- You have a hard time connecting with your baby.
- It is difficult to sleep even when the baby is sleeping.
- Anxiety and worried thoughts about your baby plague your waking hours.
- Feelings of guilt (about not being a good enough mother) overwhelm you.

In fathers, be on the lookout for:

- You feel confusion and fear.
- You suffer from irritability and frequent mood changes.
- You display negative parenting behavior.
- You have begun to withdraw from family, social, and work life.
- You are experiencing more matrimonial skirmishes.

The most severe symptoms in both mothers and fathers include:

- You are hearing voices.
- You are having suicidal thoughts.
- You have thoughts about hurting your baby.

Naturally, these thoughts can be unsettling. If you are having any of these symptoms, it is important to seek treatment with a healthcare provider or a therapist. The best way you can look after yourself if you are experiencing postpartum depression is resting as much as you can, socializing when possible, and asking for help from family and friends.

### Sleep Deprivation and Parenting

Research indicates that lack of sleep can possibly impact positive parenting (PMC, 2020). What is positive parenting? It revolves around being warm, nurturing, present, attentive, and responsive towards your baby. When we sleep less, we tend to be less focused but more stressed and high-strung. Increased levels of stress lead to a difficulty in regulating emotions. This difficulty highlights why parents who have less disjointed sleep or take longer to fall asleep display fewer positive signs of parenting around an hour before their baby's bedtime as opposed to parents who get better sleep.

### Sleep Deprivation for Children and Infants

Newborn babies spend 70% of their time sleeping. By now we know what amazing benefits a healthy sleep entails for adults. But let us not forget how essential sleep is for a child as well. Sleep for babies is beneficial because it:

- promotes growth
- helps the heart
- affects weight
- helps beat germs
- reduces injury risk
- increases attention span
- boosts learning

During Ava's time, I noticed I was better at regulating my sleeping pattern, as was Mirabelle. This in turn, helped Ava's sleeping patterns. When Ava started sleeping more, she was fresher, more active, and less cranky. Not only was this great for Ava's well-being, but it was also lovely for us to see how impactful good sleep can be for both parents and children.

SLEEP TRAINING LIKE A PRO | 27

## SLEEP HYGIENE FOR NEW PARENTS

Following are a few tips and tricks you can use to achieve better sleeping patterns and habits as a new parent.

▶ **Keep your baby near you.**

General advice regarding this is that babies should sleep in the same room as their parents for the first six months at least. This is also known as co-sleeping. Why? Well, this reassures parents about the baby's well-being which leads to decreased anxiety and better sleep. While co-sleeping does have advantages, it does have drawbacks as well. It is recommended that after six months, you transition the baby to a new room which helps everyone sleep better.

▶ **Establish a regular routine.**

When babies are born, they cannot tell the difference from night and day; hence, they will not have established internal sleep clocks. This is a learned habit. Thus, having a consistent bedtime routine for your baby helps in establishing a flow and rhythm for sleeping. If your partner is helping in caring for your baby, you can plan who will wake up in the night to help the other sleep through the night. Since I had a two-month paternity leave, I was able to help Mirabelle frequently with feeding the baby (with pumped breast milk) through the night, which helped her get a better night's sleep. Then, when she woke up refreshed, I got a chance to sleep. Taking turns was beneficial for all of us.

▶ **Keep calm and carry on.**

Coming home with a new baby—or even adding a new baby to your existing brood—can be overwhelming and chaotic. However, remember to find a calm space for yourself whenever you get the time. It could be anything from yoga, meditation, journaling, exercising, reading, catching up with a friend, or watching your favorite show. Remember, if you are not feeling the best, you will not be able to give the best, which I know you want to!

▶ **Lights out!**

In the 21$^{st}$ century, our mobile phones and tablets might as well be extensions of our hands. It is okay if you like to scroll, however, the blue light that is emitted from our phones, tablets, and TVs does play an important part in how we sleep. Essentially, blue light is artificial light which has a negative impact on sleep and ends up delaying the onset of REM sleep. This means you could be sleeping, but the quality of your sleep is compromised by such light.

An important tip is to not use your mobile phones or watch TV right before you sleep. Try doing the afore-mentioned at least 30 minutes before you plan on going to sleep. See how that works out for you in the long run.

When you do wake up in the night to feed your baby, make sure to have a soft nightlight rather than a harsh bright light. This is not only beneficial for you, but the baby as well because both of you will not be disturbed by the strong light, and you will have an easier time falling back to sleep.

▶ **Do not get up for every noise.**

You will naturally be more alert when your baby is not around you, and the slightest noise will have you worried. However, if it is something small, not responding right away will allow your baby to self-soothe in your absence, and they will fall asleep them-selves. This is beneficial in the long run as well.

▶ **You need a nap too.**

When your baby is napping, I implore you to take a nap yourself. A short nap of 20 to 30 minutes can help better your mood and help you feel more alert and perform better. Research demonstrates napping can reduce your stress level. Believe me when I say they are quite high when you become a parent (*Power Napping for Productivity, Stress Relief and Health*, n.d.). While there are other ways of boosting your alertness such as a strong cup of coffee, this is a natural way to boost your body so take advantage of the chance whenever you get to.

▶ **Be comfortable saying no.**

During the first few weeks and months, your family and friends will want to come meet you and your baby. However, it is advised that you turn these requests down. Yes, it may be uncomfortable saying no, but doctors suggest that before the baby's two-month shots, it is best they do not meet too many people to preserve their health. Say yes to family and friends coming over to see the baby once you and your baby have settled in at home and have established a routine.

▶ **Create a comfortable and cozy sleep environment.**

My room is my haven. I have black out curtains, a humidifier, a lavender scented diffuser, a comfortable mattress, and dim night lights. It is the perfect place to sleep. You will sleep better in a better environment. This works for the baby as well. Some tips I would like to share with you to create a comfortable sleep environment are as follows:

- Regulate the room temperature; it should not be too warm or too cold.
- Make the nursery dark during sleep time.
- Create a nighttime ritual which includes the baby and both parents, such as reading a bedtime story.

▶ **Do not be shy asking for help.**

Sometimes, asking for help can be the solution to your problems. Do not hesitate to ask your family and friends for help whenever you are feeling overwhelmed or sleep deprived. As the Swahili proverb goes, "Unity is strength, division is weakness."

When you ask for help, you end up making time for yourself which you can use to take a quick nap, go for a walk outdoors, or enjoy a nice long shower. These are great mood boosters. Moreover, make a timetable with your partner which works for both of you in terms of the division of responsibilities.

▶ **Take therapy.**

Yes, we do not have as much free time as we did before, however seeking therapy helps create a space solely focused on you, which is needed in busy parenting life. This time allows you to talk about yourself which is better for your mental health and functioning.

You may feel that your sleep deprivation is overwhelming. You may feel lost or angry but remember you will get through this. Live in the present, laugh at the silly instances, and take out time for yourself. Do not be hard on yourself because all of us are work in progress.

# 2

# DECODING SLEEP

One day when I returned home late from work, Mirabelle had already put Mercy to sleep. Since I had not seen or interacted much with her that day, I decided to give my daughter a goodnight kiss, and I headed toward the nursery. When I gently pushed the door open and tiptoed into seven-month-old Mercy's nursery toward her crib, her tiny blue eyes fluttered open, and my heart jumped. I thought to myself, Mirabelle will not be happy about this. I thought I had followed the correct protocol—be silent as a church mouse and do not move too much. But alas! It was then that I realized babies are the lightest sleepers. After learning my lesson, I made sure not to repeat such incidents with Ava and Mia.

Yes, there was an immense amount of love and joy when Mercy was born, but we had our fair share of shocking revelations and lessons (like the lesson I learned that day). With the addition of Ava and Mia, we learned even more about parenting. But the reality is you never stop learning. Each day brings something new, especially when you are a father to three adorable and loving children.

Before they are born, you imagine babies to be peaceful and quiet. However, when they enter this world, they enter with a bang, and that is the moment you enter the world of sleep deprivation and preoccupation. If you thought you had limited free time before, then just wait until you become a new parent.

Being a parent to a child is the most beautiful experience. While it is filled with ups and downs, it is also heartwarming and wholesome. All it takes is a smile from your child to make everything better. Things I learned while caring for my newborn daughters made the experience easier. I recommend you take the same learning opportunities and put the knowledge you gain to good use. One such useful piece of information is that babies and adults experience sleep differently. To better understand how babies sleep, you must first understand sleep cycles.

## WHAT IS THE SLEEP CYCLE?

You are passed out in a deep sleep in your comfortable bed. You may not know this (I certainly did not), but you are going through numerous 90-minute sleep cycles. The sleep cycle is a fluctuation between the slow-wave and REM phases of your sleep. Simply put, they are stages of your sleep, and ideally, you need four to six cycles of sleep every 24 hours to feel refreshed and rested.

## WHAT ARE THE SLEEP STAGES, AND WHY DO THEY MATTER?

If you did not know, sleep has four stages—three stages of non-REM sleep and one stage of REM sleep. Did you know before the discovery of REM sleep in the 1950s, sleep was thought to be a passive state during which the mind shuts down? In fact, it is quite the opposite. Scientists found that our minds are active while we sleep, working for our memories, regulating our metabolism, and removing toxins from the brain. Do you see why sleep is so important? Our health literally depends upon on it.

Sleep architecture refers to the way in which sleep is structured and categorized. Healthy sleep consists of four stages. The first three stages are NonREM1 (N1),

NonREM2 (N2), and NonREM3 (N3). The last stage is the REM stage. These four stages make one sleep cycle which is 90 minutes long. We need four cycles per night which takes seven to eight hours per night.

Each stage has its own unique purpose, fulfilling a distinct physiological and psychological function, and they occur in the same sequence. The Non-REM stages of sleep are similar to one another. During these stages our eyes move minimally or not at all, and our muscles can move but they typically do not. Our brain waves are less active and our breathing, blood pressure, and heart rate are all low in the N stages. Conversely, during REM sleep our eyes move rapidly, our muscles are mostly (or totally) paralyzed, and we have vivid dreams. During REM sleep our brain waves are actually similar to our brain waves while we are awake, which makes the stage closest to wakefulness.

### *Non-REM 1*

The N1 stage occurs when we are transitioning from wakefulness to sleep. This stage usually begins within minutes of lying down but can take longer depending on sleep habits, disorders, disturbances, and each person's unique physiology. Once the stage begins, it lasts anywhere between 1 and 7 minutes; it is short. There is some awareness of environment, but most people begin to lose their sense of time and place during this stage. During the N1 stage, the following physiological changes occur:

- Eyes close.
- Muscles begin to relax.
- Core body temperature decreases.
- Melatonin is released.
- Brain waves shift from relaxation alpha waves to the theta waves of sleep.
- You may start dreaming.

During sleep, our brain can shift from alpha waves to theta waves, and we might not even know that we are asleep. It is quite easy to be disturbed during this state —even by ourselves. Hypnic jerks and sleep starts can occur during this stage.

These are sudden contractions of the muscle that can wake us up. Sometimes it is accompanied by a sense of falling or tripping, but this is still considered normal. However, they can be worsened by caffeine, stress, and medication. Scientists believe hypnic jerks stem from our early history when we slept in trees. These sleep starts kept us from falling. Difficulty in entering N1 stage is a common symptom of insomnia. Conversely, skipping this stage and going to the REM state is a form of narcolepsy.

### *Non-REM 2*

Next, is the N2 state. About half of the four cycles of sleep is spent in this stage—making it the longest. Though the stage is similar to N1, there are some key changes that occur:

- Eye movement stops.
- There is a reduction in environmental stress.
- Heart rate and body temperature lower.
- Muscles tense and relax.
- Upper airway muscles relax.

If you talk in your sleep, it most likely occurs in N1 or N2 when you are closest to wakefulness. An important event that happens in the N2 stage is sleep spindles which are 1 to 2 second bursts of activity which results from interactions between thalamic and cortical neurons.

To help you picture it, imagine a picture of the brain. The neurons from the thalamus (located near the center) and neurons from cortex (near the top) start to interact with one another to create these sleep spindles. These spindles are essential for forming memories and remembering dreams. They also help transfer short term memories to long term memory storage.

Another brain activity seen during N2 is the occurrence of K-complexes. These are brain waves generated in the cortex that last for more than half a second and can be seen on an electroencephalography (EEG). They help us process information and synchronize sleep stages. They help us sleep by preventing us from waking up to non-threatening stimuli. However, too much time spent in this phase can indicate a sleep disorder such as sleep apnea, insomnia, or restless leg syndrome.

### Non-REM3

The N3 stage is the last non-REM stage and is commonly referred to as slow wave sleep. It usually starts about 40 minutes after falling asleep and is the most restorative of the sleep stages. It is a deep stage of sleep, and it is difficult to be woken up during this time. If you wake during this stage, you will most likely feel groggy, and your mental performance will be slower for about 30 minutes due to reduced cerebral blood flow during this stage. Other physiological changes that occur during this stage are:

- The body releases hormones that help with appetite control.
- Blood flow to the muscle increases.
- Blood pressure and heart rate decrease further.

- Memories consolidate even further.
- Breathing becomes slower.
- Sleep spindle activity decreases.

This stage is essential for our body's recovery and helps with the growth and repair of bones, muscles, and tissues. It is also essential for supporting our immune system. Furthermore, individuals who do not get enough N3 sleep may experience reduced capability to consolidate memories.

### *REM*

The final and most interesting stage of the sleep cycle is the REM sleep stage. The shift to REM sleep is different from the shifts between the first three phases. Though REM stage is the last, it is the lightest stage of sleep after N1 which means that you can be aroused in this phase more easily than all the other stages. REM sleep is characterized by:

- Body movements indicate transition out of N3 sleep.
- There is paralysis of muscles.
- Rapid and random eye movement begins.
- There are fluctuations in breathing circulations and body temperature which are unique to

REM sleep and do not occur in other sleep stages.

- Vivid dreams begin.

During the non-REM stages the mind is restful, but during REM sleep the mind is active. Brain waves are similar to those of when we are awake. Your REM stage gets longer with each sleep cycle. Interestingly, although REM sleep is most similar to physiologically being awake, it is the furthest stage from wakefulness in the sleep cycle. In fact, only babies and individuals suffering from narcolepsy can go straight from being awake to REM sleep. For most, non-REM stages of sleep must precede REM sleep.

As a sleep cycle repeats throughout the night, you spend a different amount of time in the non-REM and REM sleep stages. Typically, in the first two sleep cycles, more time is spent in non-REM sleep while subsequent cycles tend to have more time in the REM stage of sleep. Additionally, the amount of time you spend in each cycle depends on when you go to sleep. Those individuals who sleep early spend more time in non-REM sleep since it tends to be dominant between 11 p.m. to 3 a.m. Those who go to bed late and wake up late spend more time in REM sleep which occurs more often between 3 a.m. and 7 a.m. This has to do with our circadian rhythm which is our body's internal clock that regulates our sleep wake cycle. Also, REM sleep decreases as we age. Babies spend up to 50% of their time asleep in REM, while adults spend 20% of their time asleep in this stage.

To feel well rested and enjoy all the health benefits of sleep, your sleep must be sufficient and efficient. This means the completion of each stage and multiple cycles. Failure to achieve REM sleep can lead to fatigue, cognitive impairment, reduced immunity, and impaired hormone production. It can also cause changes in metabolism and heighten the risk of neurological disorders like dementia.

An inefficient sleep cycle can lead to the same consequences as sleep deprivation, such as reduced concentration and hand to eye coordination, daytime sleepiness, and irritability.

## WHAT AFFECTS SLEEP STAGES?

Sleep is valuable to all of us, and by now, I am sure you are aware of the numerous benefits a good night's sleep. However, there are some factors that do play a role in determining our sleep cycles and stages, and they can either help or hinder the effectiveness of our sleep. Following are some factors that affect sleep stages.

- **Age**: As mentioned, babies spend around 50% more time in REM sleep as opposed to adults. Hence, as we grow older, we tend to spend less time in the REM stage.
- **Recent Sleep Patterns:** If an individual has inconsistent or insufficient sleep over a period of days or longer, it could lead to them developing an unhealthy and abnormal sleep cycle.
- **Alcohol:** This should be a no-brainer. Drugs and alcohol affect our sleep architecture. Alcohol decreases REM sleep earlier in the night but once the effects start wearing off, REM sleep rebounds with longer stages in subsequent cycles.
- **Caffeine:** Just like alcohol, caffeine does not help an efficient sleep cycle. Since caffeine blocks adenosine receptors (a sleep-promoting chemical), sleep wavers and can be delayed.
- **Sleep Disorders:** Disorders such as sleep apnea, restless leg syndrome, and other conditions can affect sleep cycles and stages.

In the next few chapters, I am going to cover sleep patterns, sleep habits, sleep facts, and sleep methods and tricks for different age groups that will help you train your child to sleep better.

3

# HOW NEWBORNS SLEEP

When Mercy was born, Mirabelle and I had to forego the luxury of consistent and undisturbed sleep. We woke up groggy and disoriented through the night and would dream of a good night's sleep. Not only did we have to adjust to Mercy's sleeping patterns but our own new patterns as well. Moreover, when I returned to work after my paternity leave ended, it was difficult to adjust yet again. Between 0 to 3 months, I can guarantee Mirabelle and I were the most sleep deprived we have ever been.

When my paternity leave ended, I would head to work like a zombie, make myself a strong shot of espresso, and get ready for the day ahead of me. One of my colleagues, Ahmed, who happens to be a good friend of mine, helped support me during my "nocturnal days."

There were days when he would cover for me and days when he would give me a pep talk on how this was a passing phase. Honestly, having a support system was helpful; it just made those daunting days easier.

Ahmed's family moved to the USA from Pakistan when he was five years old, and his parenting tips were so helpful with Mercy. He encouraged me to reach out to my family or Mirabelle's family members to ask for help whenever we felt overwhelmed. Many countries like Nigeria, Ghana, Pakistan, China, Cameroon, etc. embrace the concept of joint family systems. A new mother usually has her in-laws at home to offer support, which makes it slightly easier for new parents. Luckily, by the time Ava and Mia were born, we had learned enough through experience and reading about babies' sleeping patterns.

If I were to give you one valuable tip, it would be to prepare with your own research on sleeping patterns of babies, so you can better manage your time when you become a parent for the first (or second) time. When we did, it was a great game-changer for Mirabelle and I. Life became much easier and manageable. You may think your baby's sleep pattern is erratic or disorganized, but it is not. There is a science behind it. While their cycle will not be the same as yours, you need to know that they do have a sleep cycle. Before we dive into sleep training your baby, let us look at how babies' sleep cycles work.

## NEWBORNS: 0-3 MONTHS

The hours of sleep children need differs depending on the individual and certain aspects—including age. It varies each month. Babies' sleep patterns change from right when they are born until they are about one and half to two-years-old. Newborn babies do not have an internal clock or a circadian rhythm like adults do; hence, their sleep patterns are not in sync to daylight or nighttime.

### How Much Sleep do They Need?

Sleep for the baby is important in the early years, especially for the overall development of the baby, such as the brain and body. A lot of healthy development takes place during this time, so babies sleep a good amount. They usually sleep for 18 to 20 hours during their first three months (known as the phase of transition). When the baby comes out of the womb—a completely different environment—and into this world, they need time to adjust. Mercy slept for at least 20 hours a day initially, but that gradually decreased over time.

There are no nap schedules for the first three months, as your infant should be allowed to sleep on demand. A baby usually wakes up for 45 minutes to an hour during this age. When your baby is 1 to 4 weeks old, they may sleep at least 15 to 20 hours a day. However, this is often in doses of fragmented periods. As babies advance in age, the effort needed to put them back to sleep will change. Parents must adjust to this change if they want their baby to have a good sleep schedule. Keep in mind, premature babies may sleep longer, while babies with colic may sleep less.

### Sleep Habits and Patterns

I would like to bust a myth surrounding babies' sleeping patterns. It seems many believe babies should quickly reach the stage of sleeping through the night without any crying. However, this is not correct. As a parent, it is our responsibility to debunk these myths and not take night waking as a failure on our part.

The fact is that your baby is supposed to sleep a lot in the initial months. However, since newborn babies have a small tummy, you cannot feed them at bedtime and expect them to sleep during the night. Newborns need to be fed at least every two to four hours, which includes throughout the night as well. The trick here is learning to decipher your baby's cries. This will take some time, but you will get there. Then, when your baby is hungry, you can respond by feeding them as opposed to responding to random noises in their sleep.

Another important thing to know is that they are restless sleepers. While adults can sleep for hours at a time, babies squiggle around and wake up frequently during their sleep. This is in part because half of their sleep is spent in the REM stage, which as you know, is the phase of your sleep where you have vivid dreams and are closest to wakefulness. However, do not lose hope. Your baby will mature, as will their sleeping patterns, and eventually they will enjoy a deeper and undisturbed sleep.

Newborn babies are not the quietest or most peaceful sleepers. Your little bundle will most probably be a noisy sleeper the first few months after being born. A newborn baby has irregular breathing consisting of strange noises and short pauses. As a new parent, it is natural to be alarmed, but it is nothing to worry about. Rather, it is better to be informed about your newborn's respiratory growth. A newborn's usual breathing rate is around 40 to 60 breaths a minute while they are awake. This rate may drop down to 30 to 40 breaths per minute once they fall asleep. They might even take shallow and fast breaths for nearly 15 to 20 seconds, followed by a complete pause during in which they stop breathing completely for a few seconds. A newborn has an undeveloped breathing-control center in their brain. Do not worry; this is a natural process. Your baby will make rattling, whistling, and gurgling noises as well. However, it may be cause for concern if you notice any of the following:

- Your baby is grunting after each and every breath.
- You notice their nostrils flaring, which indicates your baby is working extra hard to get air.
- Your baby's breathing is rapid (up to more than 70 breaths per minute) for an extended time.
- You see the muscles between their ribs retract, which indicates a struggle to breath.

Remember, your baby will confuse night and day. They were in complete darkness, while in your womb, for nine whole months. Your womb provided a place to snooze the entire day while you were busy and active. Your baby's circadian rhythm has not kicked in yet, which means their body clock has not set itself. Thankfully, a newborn's nocturnal habits are only temporary, and once they come into this world, they begin to adjust and will become accustomed to the difference between day and night. You can help this process along as well. To regulate and kick start your baby's circadian rhythm, make sure to do the following:

- Allow your baby to spend time in sunlight or natural light while awake.
- Aim to make your baby's awake time interactive and bright.
- Put them to sleep in a dark room with white noise.
- Before bedtime, keep stimulation to a minimum.

Finally, you need to know that your sleep habits will affect your baby's sleep habits. Well-rested parents are more present and better at regulating moods and emotions. If you are not well rested, you will likely be more irritated putting your baby to sleep. As babies can pick up on your emotions and stress, this will only make the process more difficult. As I always say, it is important to take good care of yourself. Follow my philosophy of inside out. Take care of your needs first and then work outwards. You will notice a considerable change in the quality of the care you give out as well.

### *Help Your Baby Sleep Better*

Considering how much newborns sleep during their first three months, you might imagine they would be fresh and ready to take on the world. Unfortunately, that is not the case. Babies in this age bracket overtire easily; hence, they need to switch off and sleep. Because of this, some parents might simply cut down the awake time between naps. However, this might backfire. Your baby will be unsettled, will end up crying more, and may wake up frequently during the night. This is because your baby is now under tired. Yes, being under tired is a real thing!

During the first three months, I can guarantee your baby will be waking up every two to three hours for milk. It is rare for a newborn to sleep through the night up until 6 months. However, besides waking up for milk, your baby may also wake up due to the following reasons:

- They are not swaddled in the correct manner. Swaddling helps to suppress the startle reflex, which is vital to your baby sleeping better.
- Environmental or household noises are a disturbance to them.
- Their body temperature is either too hot or cold.
- They are not feeling well.
- They have reflux.
- They may have had too little or too much sleep.

You must be wondering how on earth you will decipher what your baby is really feeling? Well, you will learn and decode, so be patient and go with the flow. Once you learn and understand what your baby needs, you will be better able to anticipate and answer them. This will eventually help everyone sleep better.

I know it sounds daunting when you hear or read about babies needing to be fed throughout the night, but the good news is that it will not last for very long. Mirabelle did have a difficult time initially, which is completely okay. She was moody, sleep deprived, and exhausted, but she did eventually settle into a pattern. More importantly, I was there to help her and act as a strong support system. If you are a father reading this, please make it a priority to support to your partner when it comes to taking care of your baby.

Newborns go through a period of adjusting and settling. You see, their brains work in different ways than ours and are changing rapidly. By four months, you will notice your baby's sleep cycle will start to match an adult's sleep cycle. They will begin to move through more of the sleep stages much like adults do. This period is known as the 4-month sleep regression. When babies start to fully wake up in between sleep cycles, they will need help going back to sleep. This can be every 35-45 minutes during the day and every two hours during the night.

Prior to this age, a baby tends to drift more easily between sleep cycles during their day naps or night sleep. Hence, the way you put your baby to sleep before 12 weeks will not have much of an impact on how long they will stay asleep. There is no concept of "spoiling" your baby during this time, but there is no harm in cultivating a healthy sleeping pattern as it will be beneficial later.

You can establish a healthy routine by doing the following:

- Try to put your baby to sleep for a nap in their bed, at least once a day, so they can learn and familiarize themselves with their eventual sleeping place.
- Try to put your baby to sleep in your bed rather than your arms, so they know this is where they must sleep.
- Allow the baby to fall asleep on their own if you think they are ready.

It goes without saying that the environment your baby sleeps in will have an impact on the type of sleep they have. In their newborn phase, they can nod off just about anywhere and everywhere. One of the most important factors to consider during this phase is how well they are swaddled. A good and tight swaddle will help your baby sleep longer. Swaddling is one of the best and oldest tricks in the book of sleep for newborns. Since swaddling replicates the feeling of a confined and warm womb, it ensures the newborn they are safe and warm.

Another vital component in helping your baby settle and sleep better is white noise. Since your baby is used to noise as loud as a vacuum cleaner during the entire day in your tummy (the sound your digestive system, heartbeat, and blood pumping), white noise will be familiar and comforting for them. It will help them fall asleep easily. You can play it loudly during daytime naps and nighttime sleep.

When your baby is 8 weeks old, you will observe changes in them which signal a shift in their hormonal balance—their hormones from birth will start wearing off. Their body will start producing Melatonin which is responsible for helping us sleep. This hormone is only produced and released in the dark; hence, putting your baby to sleep in a dark room will do wonders for a good night's sleep. You may not know this, I certainly did not, but babies find the dark comforting. They are not scared of the dark as grown children or even some adults are. This is because newborns do not have the space to feel emotions such as fear. Thus, I would advise you not to use night lights since it may stimulate your baby right before sleeping.

## NEWBORNS: 3-6 MONTHS

This is a big jump from the 0-3 month sleeping patterns and habits. Months 3-6 can be quite tricky. Since your baby's sleep patterns are undergoing such a drastic change, you will have to readjust and tweak a few things here and there. You will observe how your baby's sleep will slowly start resembling an adult's sleep —marked by neurologically segregated sleep cycles. During this period:

- Your baby's daytime sleep cycle will not be as advanced as it will be later.
- Your baby will not solely depend on sleep cues or certain behaviors to sleep.
- Your baby's sleep cycle will become more organized.
- Sleep becomes a conscious factor, and it will take practice to nail it.
- Your baby will begin to wake up fully in between each sleep cycle rather than transitioning from one cycle to the other automatically.
- If your baby is used to you feeding or rocking them to sleep, they will expect and rely on you to do the same between each cycle when they wake. This will be around every 35-45 minutes

during the day and two hours during the night.

- If your baby doesn't self-settle (self-soothe) after this cycle, they will eventually be overtired in the evening.

By the time your baby hits the three-month mark, they will be sleeping around 15 hours during the day. They will generally have 3.5 hours of daytime sleep, spread across three different nap times. They will need around 2-2.5 hours of awake time between each nap. Overnight sleep will be around 12 hours.

### How Much Sleep do They Need?

Now, you may find yourself asking the million-dollar question: how much sleep should a 3–6-month baby really get, including naps? Well, simply put, it depends on the age of your baby. The following chart will help you understand better.

| Age | Total Daytime Sleep (approx.) | Naps | Length |
| --- | --- | --- | --- |
| 3-4 months | 3 ¼ hours | X3 | Between 15/45 mins - 2.5 hours |
| 4-6 months | 3 hours | X3 | Between 10/15 mins - 2.5 hours |

In reference to this chart, your 3-month-old baby should be getting around 3.5 hours of daytime sleep, spread out in three naps, one in the morning, lunchtime, and afternoon, from 7 a.m. to 7 p.m. When your baby is five-months-old, you will notice that they may start to resist their third (afternoon time) nap. However, this does not mean they are completely ready to let go of it. Up until 6 months, the late afternoon nap is important, even as it shortens in duration. It will ensure that your baby is not over tired at bedtime and will not be restless throughout the night.

Nap times vary throughout the day. However, it is essential to establish and keep a consistent pattern of long and restorative two-hour naps in the middle of the day when your baby will feel a natural dip in their energy. This can also be a good time for you to have some shut eye, since adults feel a slump in their energy at this time as well.

One of the main reasons to aim for this restorative two-hour nap is that babies enter the REM phase. During the REM phase, a lot happens for the baby, such as the regulation of their appetite, emotions, reduced stress, reduced cortisol levels, consolidation of new memories and skills, boosted immune system, and strengthening of connections in the brain. If that is not enough evidence to get your baby to take a two hour restorative nap, then I do not know what is.

While it has been established that napping is para-mount to your baby's health, it is also essential to high-light that your baby needs the right amount of awake time. Too much of awake time will naturally lead to over tiredness, where too little of awake time will lead to under tiredness. Both scenarios will lead to bad nap times and bad nighttime sleep, which will equate to a very cute but grumpy baby and a very irritable and moody parent.

Between 3-6 months, your baby has a greater need for awake time than when they are newly born. By now, your baby will be more aware of their surroundings, will want to play, and will need visual stimulation. If you are trying to put them to sleep after only an hour of them being awake, you will face a lot of resistance and will have to put in extra rocking and feeding time. For your information, 3–6-month-old babies need about 2-2.5 hours of awake time between each nap they take. This time works out well with their entire sleep schedule.

While sleep is great, it is important to look out for signs that your baby is oversleeping during the 3–6-month period. As discussed previously, a lot of day sleep can lead to night waking and your baby being restless. However, if you are noticing that your baby is sleeping more than usual throughout the day, there may be some reasons behind this.

- **Illness:** This is the top reason your baby could be sleeping more than usual. If your baby is unwell, it can cause chaos to their sleep routine in the form of waking up from naps and waking up during the night. However, sleeping more than the required amount is also an indication that your baby's body is fighting off the illness.
- **Growth Spurt:** When babies grow, they begin to take longer than usual naps and sleep later in the morning. During the first 6 months, you will notice that your baby will go through a lot of sleepy phases, during which they will seem to be sleeping around the clock.

If your 3–6-month-old baby is sleeping like a new-born baby, please do consult a pediatrician.

### *Sleep Habits and Patterns*

Due to sleep regressions, babies will have to relearn sleep skills periodically since parts of their brain responsible for sleep are continually maturing and evolving. As I mentioned before, by the time your baby turns four-months-old, they will begin to wake up fully in between each sleep cycle. Sleep regression lingers until your baby learns how to self-settle. This simply means your baby will be able to sleep on their own when they are ready. Self-soothing does not happen in a day. Since is it a novel concept for babies, they will need help, consistency, and practice.

By now, you will want to establish a healthy and consistent routine for your baby. It does not have to be an army regimented routine; all you must do is provide structure. As Michael Hyatt said, "Consistency is better than perfection. We can all be consistent, perfection is impossible."

Structures and routines are a part of everyone's life. Mirabelle and I had our morning five-minute meditation and coffee routine during the years when we were raising our three children. Even when things seemed to be chaotic all around, our morning ritual of a cup of coffee and five minutes of mindful silence and meditation really helped us. Mirabelle's friend, Akari, recommended a famous Zen meditation practiced in Japan, called Zazen meditation. It proved to be helpful. It requires one to sit in a quiet and clean place. You must sit on your knees, with your back straight, chin up as if you are trying to reach high, all while breathing in slowly and letting your thoughts flow. I cannot begin to tell you how beneficial these five minutes of meditation were for my mental health. It is a small act of following a routine, making a space for yourself, and allowing yourself silence in an otherwise noisy and busy day.

Routines provide comfort and familiarity, and it is wonderful to give the same to your baby. Remember to feed them and have them nap at the same time every day. You should also know how important naps are for your baby's growth and development. They are as important as milk is nutritious for them. For them to have a good night's sleep, they need to take naps during the day. There should be a good balance between day and night sleep. Very little day sleep leads to cortisol (a stress hormone) building up in your baby which makes it more difficult for them to settle down. This causes them to wake up during the night and extremely early in the morning. Now, we don't want that, do we? Always remember that naps are important.

I will give you a minute-to-minute breakdown of what their daytime and nighttime sleep cycle can look like. This will help you understand your baby's sleep pattern better. The daytime sleep cycle follows the following routine:

- **0-10 Minutes:** Your baby will start falling asleep and will enter a light sleep stage. Your baby can be woken up easily by a noise or being put down from your arms.

- **10-20 Minutes:** Your baby will enter the deep sleep stage and will now be unaware of their surroundings.
- **20-30 Minutes:** Now your baby is fast asleep, and their breathing is regulated and deep. This is the restorative phase of their sleep cycle.
- **30-40 Minutes:** Your baby will now begin to stir out their deep sleep and can be fully awake by this point.
- **40-45 Minutes:** This period marks the end of your baby's sleep cycle.

Your baby's nighttime sleep cycle will naturally be longer than their daytime sleep cycle. Their nighttime sleep cycle will consist of the following pattern:

- **45 Minutes After Bedtime:** If your baby is under tired, over tired, ill, or uneasy, they will most probably wake up at this time.
- **2 Hours After Bedtime:** Your baby will most probably stir out of their first nighttime cycle at this point. They will enter a deep sleep phase until midnight. During this stage, your baby will not wake up unless they are feeling sick or hungry.
- **Midnight:** By midnight, your baby's deep sleep phase will end, and they will enter a lighter

sleep phase. They are more likely to be woken if they are hungry, cold, ill, uneasy, and under or overtired.

- **Every 2 Hours:** Your baby's sleep cycle is two hours long; hence, the cycle will continue. Some babies may need help being put back to sleep during this time if they cannot self-settle.
- **5 a.m.:** The probability of your baby waking up during this hour is the highest. If they do wake up at this time, it is difficult to put them back to sleep, especially if they had a good night's sleep.

### *Help Your Baby Sleep Better*

Now it is time to get your baby ready for bed. For them to have a good night's sleep, we need to have the perfect environment.

Right before each nap, you can read them a story, sing a lullaby, change their diaper, cuddle them, and put them in a swaddle. These acts will calm your baby and are great cues for them to get ready for naptime. By replicating these steps in the same order, your baby will get used to them and will know that it is time for them to sleep. For their nighttime routine, you can build a schedule that works for you and your baby. For example:

- **6:00 p.m.:** Help your baby relax with a warm bath.
- **6:10 p.m.:** After drying your baby, message them with some natural oil.
- **6:10 p.m.:** Dress your baby in their sleeping clothes and sing a lullaby or read a story to them.
- **6:15-30 p.m.:** Begin bedtime milk feeding.
- **6:50 p.m.:** When bedtime milk feeding ends, give your baby a warm cuddle and sing them a lullaby. Put your baby in bed for the night.
- **7:00 p.m.:** Your baby goes to bed awake but sleepy, and they are ready to sleep through the night.

This is a perfect situation in an ideal world with no obstructions. In the real world, you may come across hurdles, such as your baby being tired, cranky, an unexpected visitor, or unforeseen loud noises. So, be prepared for them.

Knowing your baby's sleep patterns and how to manage them will make life much easier for you. By knowing about the sleep patterns, you will be better able to use any tips and techniques to establish a healthy sleep schedule and ways to overcome irregularities in sleep structures.

# 4

# HOW INFANTS SLEEP

By sixth months, babies' sleep cycles start to resemble an adult's sleep cycle more closely, but they aren't quite there yet. Since they do not need to be fed as frequently, they tend to sleep throughout the night, giving everyone a chance to catch some undisturbed shut eye. I told you there would be light at the end of the tunnel. While their sleep patterns may have seemed erratic and tough to cope with, during this period the baby adopts a more systemic sleep pattern. It is advised that parents be responsive to their baby's needs which promotes responsive settling within the baby. In simpler terms, responsive settling is identifying and acknowledging that your baby needs help and responding in a suitable manner.

## HOW MUCH SLEEP DO THEY NEED?

As the days advance, and your baby enters their sixth month, they should be getting an average of around 11 hours of sleep, along with 3.5-hour naps spaced throughout the day—morning, afternoon, and late afternoon. By the time they turn nine-months-old, they will be sleeping an average of 11 hours throughout the night. However, nap time will decrease slightly, and naps will be cut down from three in a day to two in a day.

In total, your baby will be getting around 13 hours of sleep over a period of 24 hours. Not only is this great for the baby, but it is a wonderful time for you to take things slower and make time for yourself. If your baby is napping, watch a show, read a book, exercise, or nap yourself. Small doses of activity solely focused on yourself will give you a renewed energy and will leave you feeling fresher throughout the day.

By this age, babies will only wake up once through the night and will need the parent to settle them back to sleep. Waking up once is an average estimate; however, your baby may wake up more than once. By this age, most babies are ready to sleep between 6 p.m. and 10 p.m. It can take less than 40 minutes to put your baby to sleep, but around 1 in 10 babies take longer to fall asleep. Physically, your baby is prepared for this shift (sleeping through the night), but they may not be ready emotionally since they are used to feeding and cuddling during the course of the night.

## SLEEP HABITS AND PATTERNS

By now your baby knows the difference between day and night. Between 6 months to a year, your baby will start to feel distress when you leave—even for a short while. This is because your baby has begun to associate you with care and safety. This is known as person permanence. This does not mean you cannot leave their sight; that would be impossible and unhealthy. Instead, just know that because your baby wants to stay close to you, they may cry when separated from you. This is known as separation anxiety. Separation anxiety can cause your child to take longer to fall asleep.

You must remember that you cannot be with your child physically around the clock. When you are not around your baby, they will learn to self-soothe, which is an important component in their development. If you find that your baby is waking up more than usual through the night, you can help your baby settle. Following are a few tips you can follow to settle your baby:

- Acknowledge and answer their tired signs.
- Use constant and positive bedtime routines.
- Establish your presence to make your baby feel safe and secure by sleeping in their room.
- Camp out (stick around) in the nursery until your baby falls asleep.

You know yourself and your baby best, hence you will better be able to figure out what works for you and your baby. While sleep seems so natural and something we are so used to, it can often be the most challenging part of parenting. For babies between 6-12 months, sleep is critical for their development and well-being. Remember, as a parent it is imperative to manage your expectations—nothing will happen in one shot. Normalize experiences and be patient with yourself. During this stage, you can be aware of the following factors:

- While sleep does stretch out for your baby during this time, it does not always coincide with the parents sleep. Maybe your baby is getting a good stretch but not in the time frame you like. Make sure their sleep cycle and rhythm matches their circadian rhythm. Even at 6-months make sure they are getting a good amount of sunshine. It would be nice to have a

window open in the morning. I used to do a
dramatic wake up for Ava. I would go into her
nursery with a song and open the window. I did
not startle her but roused her gently from her
sleep. All that light is important during the day,
and a dark room at night is good.

- During this time in your baby's life, tummy
  time is important because it helps with motor
  skills and development. Watch their daytime
  calories. Sometimes they can reverse their
  eating and end up eating more at night. This is
  because they ate a certain way during the first
  4-5 months, and now they must adjust to a
  different set of eating patterns. It will take time;
  just make sure your baby is getting enough
  nutrition during the day.

- The temperature should be between 68-74
  degrees in the nursery. White noise is still good
  for your baby to hear as it screens household
  sounds out for sleeping babies. It should play all
  night long and in a low tone. (Make sure there
  is no high-pitched pinging or on/off cycling.)

- Establish a good routine. If you think about it,
  when you tell a toddler it is time to leave the
  park "right now," they most likely throw a
  tantrum because they did not get time to say
  goodbye to the slide, to the sandbox, or to the

swing. For babies you are their park, so it is a big deal for them to say goodbye to you. Have a routine. This is like their 10-minute warning to say bye for the night.

At around 6 months, they undergo a growth spurt. You will see more sleep stretches, and awake times will lengthen. Nap organization does not typically happen until after 6 months and often not until 8 months. You may notice that awake windows get longer, and the nap organization starts coming into place. When you see your baby fussy between 6 p.m. and 9 p.m. at night, it is a sign that you are probably waiting too long to put your baby to bed. You need to look at 7 a.m. to 7 p.m. as an established full day for the baby. So, around 6:30 p.m. and 7:30 p.m. (when the beginning of night sleep starts) you should be putting them to sleep.

It is a tricky season trying to learn what the ideal bedtime is; my suggestion is that you always start earlier. That can solve a lot of night awakenings and early risings. Logically, one would think if the baby were more tired they would sleep more, but that is not the case. If you miss their sleep window, you will hit their second sleep window around 9:00 p.m. This is when the cortisol kicks in, and if you try to put a baby down at that time, it is like you are going to sleep with four cups of coffee in your system—not ideal.

At this age, they are still probably taking three naps during the day. In an ideal world, that would be a one-and-a-half-hour morning nap, a one-and-a-half-hour afternoon nap, and a 30-minute top off nap—similar to the last-minute milk feed before bed. What is happening differently is that the distance between the last nap and bedtime becomes under 3 hours during this period. The last 30-minute nap is not exactly a restorative sleep, but more to top off to keep their cortisol at bay. Your goal is to have the last nap about two and a half hours before bedtime.

Unfortunately, we don't always hit the naptime sweet spot! Don't be discouraged; find the silver lining. Days when I would work from home (when Mirabelle would be overwhelmed and need help) and I was on nap duty were a great time for me to bond with my daughters. My help dissipated any marital stress between Mirabelle and I, and the girls would also sleep better since there was a calming and peaceful environment through the day.

Between 9 to 12 months, the window between the last nap and bedtime will stretch to four hours. You will often see that somewhere around 7.5 months and 8.5 months, they will drop that third nap. This can be painful for the parent because sometimes they need the third nap, and sometimes they do not. Sometimes bedtime is earlier, and sometimes it is not. You must make the shift with them. They still need 14 hours of sleep, which is considered ideal, but 11 is the minimum amount you should aim for.

During this time, you will also notice that your baby is dreaming about the things they have gone through during REM sleep, which can excite and wake them.

## SIX MONTH SLEEP REGRESSION

When you hear 6-month sleep regression, I want you to know that it actually means progress for your baby. Don't be surprised if, even after successful sleep, your baby regresses after they hit the 6-month mark. Around this time, the sleep challenges will increase. Your baby becomes more aware of their environment, they are developing physically and neurologically, exploring their skill sets, and moving around. They have a lot going on. This in turn is distracting them from falling asleep.

Some of the signs of sleep regression are:

- 5 A.M. wake ups
- shorter naps
- sleep resistance
- night waking

What causes this?

- teething
- learning to sit up by themselves
- motor skill developments

One of the things babies tend to start doing at the 6-month mark is figuring out how to go to sleep themselves. For instance, if your baby was using a sleep prop only occasionally, it will become the central focus at the 6-month mark. A sleep prop could be anything from rocking, patting, and even feeding before sleeping. Suddenly, it may seem that you must rock the baby for a full 15 minutes before they fall asleep, and transferring them to the crib is not going well either.

Props that were being used easily and only occasionally are now becoming problematic, and it is going to start taking longer and be more difficult to put the baby down. Worry not, this is a good sign! It means that your baby is outgrowing the sleep props and is most likely looking for guidance on how to fall asleep independently, but they don't know how to go about it.

Regression marks a great time to start sleep training. It takes a couple of nights for the baby to figure out what to do without props, but they will eventually resume to self-settling. This signifies that the baby was ready to find those skills.

When Mercy's six-month sleep regression began, Mirabelle and I were exhausted. I remember thinking at that time, *I just put in so much effort sleep training my baby and now there are more challenges?* But trust me. It gets better, and it is a good sign. How can you make life easier for yourself and your baby during this period?

- Assess and understand safe sleep guidelines.
- Follow a steady and consistent sleep schedule.
- Establish a bedtime routine.
- Help your baby fall asleep in their crib.
- Keep distractions to a minimum before their bedtime.
- Establish and work on a day-night distinction.

## HELP YOUR BABY SLEEP BETTER

If you are getting by with your baby's sleeping patterns, if they are not affecting you or your family negatively, and if you have a system in place which works most of the time, then know you are doing a wonderful job.

However, if your baby's sleeping patterns are impacting you, your baby, and your family negatively, then that is a cause of concern. Your baby could be going through severe night waking. This means that you baby does one or more of the following, at least five or more times, for around one to two weeks:

- Your infant consistently wakes up more than three times during the night.
- They take more than 30 minutes to settle before sleeping.
- Your infant wants to sleep in your bed.
- They have a problem sleeping and settling which causes you distress.

If this becomes difficult for you to manage, please seek professional help from a doctor.

Moreover, crying is natural for the baby. While most times you will be able to soothe them and respond to their needs, there will be days where you fail to shush them. It is okay. Go easy on yourself, ask your partner to help, reach out to your support system, and take a break for yourself. As Michelle Obama said, "To be a good parent, you need to take care of yourself so that you can have the physical and emotional energy to take care of your family."

# 5

# HOW TODDLERS SLEEP

Toddler's fall between the ages of 1 to 3-years-old. As your baby grows from an infant into a toddler, not only will you observe their physical appearance, personality, and motor skills develop, but their sleeping patterns as well.

Nobody can really prepare you for what is to come, but I want to walk you through each stage so that you are not completely surprised. When Mercy was around 14 months, we noticed such a shift in her personality and sleep patterns that Mirabelle and I asked ourselves, "Is this supposed to be happening?"

## HOW MUCH SLEEP DO THEY NEED?

By now, your toddler will have eliminated their morning and evening naps and will probably nap only once during the day. This nap could last between 1 to 2 hours. You can encourage your toddler to nap by having a quiet, consistent pre-nap routine. For example, you could sing a gentle song, have a cuddle, or read a story before naps. It's also good to make sure your toddler takes daytime naps in their crib or bed. If your toddler stops sleeping at nap time altogether, you could try enforcing a "quiet rest" at the same time each day.

Ideally, toddlers need around 14 hours of sleep a day; however, the average number they actually get could be as little as 10 hours. Typically they will fall asleep between 7 p.m. and 9 p.m. and wake up between 6 a.m. and 8 a.m. It may seem that your toddlers are having trouble getting settled before bedtime or sleeping through the night, and since they are exploring their newfound independence and movement, getting them ready for bedtime can be challenging at times.

## HOW TO HELP A TODDLER SLEEP

Toddler requests typically start small. From 18 months to 2 years, you will notice a pattern of them asking for one more drink or one more teddy. They may want mom to do one thing, and then, they want dad to do it. You will notice this may begin during the time leading up to bedtime—not necessarily at bedtime. You need to be aware and ready for these demands and questions that will come up so that you may nip it in the bud.

**Imagine this:**

It is 6:30 or 7 p.m. It is nighttime, you are exhausted, and you are done with the negotiating. At this point, you are willing to give away your soul for some peace and quiet. You find yourself tempted to give in, but you need to be mindful that by doing so, you could be starting a pattern. If your boundaries start to relax, your toddler will notice the points at which they are able to manipulate you and get that sense of control they are seeking. It could be as soon as you are on the phone or speaking to a friend. They are intelligent, and they know by your tone that you are probably just minutes away from giving in. This is when they will ask. Remember, they are not doing it out of malice, but they are hardwired to learn and explore their boundaries. It is intrinsic. It is natural for them to explore, learn, and seek.

*Strategies*

During this period their autonomy is developing, and they begin to view themselves as an individual. Your job is to recognize this early on. There are a few tips I would like to give as to how you can easily transition your toddler from the day to being ready for bedtime.

▶ **Use stamp charts.**

You do not want this to be a reward-based chart; however, you can have an element of reward. Maybe offer them a stuffed toy when they finally go to bed. To make it more adult-like, you could put it on a clipboard and allow them to place the stamp themselves. The goal is to have them stamp each activity as they go along the course of the day. This gives them a sense of control and proves to be a distraction from their usual routine. This also helps to go back to a certain activity and say, "No sweetie, we have already done this." Then, you only need to hold your ground when they ask for more of something before winding down to bedtime. Recognize that being fair and kind to both yourself and your toddler is important.

▶ **Preface bedtime routines with quality time.**

Sometimes a simple time of transition before bedtime routines begin can be helpful. It is important that this time be protected—no phones. Both partners need to be involved and extraneous distractions should be at a minimum, for whatever amount of time you can take out—even just 15 minutes. During this time, you need to be playing together and interacting meaningfully with your child because immediately after, you will be beginning the sequence of events that signals bedtime.

This strategy allows connection before direction. When you are busy cleaning from dinner or if you return from work and immediately start saying, "Get ready. It is bedtime; brush your teeth and get into your pajamas!" that will not work. We struggle with such transitions ourselves, so you can imagine what it must be like for them. It is uninviting. Adults like to slow down, take it easy, and then get ready for bed, so do the same for your toddler. Go into their nursery, play with them, and give them your undivided attention. Make bedtime playful, have a laugh, be silly and try to find fun in the process. Keep it special, it will change the whole dynamic

▶ **Stretch it out.**

Remember that by the time we hit 6 p.m. your toddler has had a full day. If you start giving them multiple directions at the end of a long day, it can be hard for them. It is difficult for toddlers' brains to be compliant to all of these directives with focus and attention. When they seem fidgety and unfocused, you may have a tendency to get annoyed. But if we leave this sequence to the end of their day, what can we expect? They are not robots!

Bedtime for toddlers may require you to alter the entire family schedule. To allow for adequate wind down, you can break the sequence up or maybe consider trying things in a different order. Maybe give a bath earlier in the evening or switch up dinner time. You could change them into their pajamas slightly earlier than you used to. These small changes can have an effect. Initially, it may seem weird to you, but eventually it can become your own unique routine.

▶ **Be flexible with daytime nap changes.**

If your toddler is heading to 2.5 and 3-years and naps are becoming difficult during daytime, be mindful of how much you push those naps. Are they ready for more awake time? Are they having milk or screen time before their nap? Look at the lead up to bedtime. There comes a point where our little ones just nod off in the car or in their stroller, and that is how parents keep a countdown till they eliminate naps completely. This is a period of about six months or more. Be prepared that jump might need to happen. If your little one is ready to stop napping, the more you push them the more they want to fuss and argue. Take the hint; the nap is not serving you or them.

*Things to Remember*

When your little one starts to notice changes to their bedtime routine, they can develop a sense of angst. You may notice more negative behaviors come into play, and they will try to control more of their time. This could be in the form of more requests or tantrums. What you need to do is make sure you are able to hold your boundaries. If children feel they are in control, you have given up yours. This communicates to them that you are no longer the parent, and they must do things themselves. This is an uncomfortable situation for everyone involved. You will notice meltdowns and anger. This is a sign that you have let your toddler take the lead. During this tricky time where they are learning the balance of control and authority, you should remember the following.

▶ **Don't undermine each other.**

Remember, when it is not your turn, allow your partner to be fully immersed in the experience and give them that responsibility. If one of you steps in during the process, this undermines the partner's role. Take a step back during that routine and give the other partner a chance to step up.

## ▶ Stand Firm

When I was on bedtime duty, I used to watch out for small requests, and if I said, "No, we have already the books," the children would express how annoyed they were at me for having held my boundary. It is not your job to fix or to make sure that they do not feel any of those emotions. Your job is to hold the space supportively and lovingly for them to let these emotions out because this will make it easier for them to realize that the boundary is there to stay. It may not feel the best for them; however, once they know they can trust your boundary, they will let go of the idea of controlling their bedtime (or whatever other issue it may be).

As a father, sometimes I gave in because of the guilt of not being able to play with them the entire day. But I soon realized that was disruptive for my daughters and ruined the concept of consistency.

We do not need to punish them at this age; they are allowed to have big emotions. Please do not say, "do not cry," or, "there is nothing to be upset about," to them. Rather, be an encourager and say, "I know you are upset. I know you wanted one more bedtime story, but mummy/daddy has already said no. I am ready when you are." Remember to do all things kindly. It will take a little while initially, maybe a few nights to get through the tantrum, but I believe in you, and you can get through it. By stopping these requests earlier on and knowing you can hold to healthy boundaries, you are building a healthy space with structure and nurturing.

#### ▶ Look out for the second wind.

What exactly is the second wind? This happens when your toddler is overtired, but their body will get a second wind. Their bodies release hormones such as adrenaline and cortisol which causes them to stay awake longer than their natural sleep window. It is also known as the *dreaded* second wind by parents since none of us are fans of it.

#### ▶ Toddlers are renowned for taking micro-opportunities to rest and recharge.

They may start to look sleepy and tired while sitting in their highchair watching TV, having screen time, enjoying milk, or simply chilling out for 15 minutes. Unfortunately, they will get right up, be done with the activity, and you will have your vivacious toddler back again. Whatever you do, you do not want them to be grossly overtired; that will impact their ability to get into a deep sleep. While avoiding the second wind, you also must balance their awake time. Be mindful of keeping them engaged while awake. Read a fun book before bed, play puzzles, or build blocks so that they may engage with you.

You must be confident in the knowledge you have when adjusting your toddler's bedtime. Make changes pleasantly. If you try to take control of bedtime but lack authority, confidence, kindness, or consistency, they will not trust you to lead or hold their space. Get back in the driver's seat.

## YOUR TODDLER'S BEDTIME ROUTINE

The evening has arrived, and it is time to get your toddler ready for bed. Most toddlers are ready for bedtime between 6:30 p.m. and 7:00 p.m. This is the ideal time because their deep sleep is between 8:00 p.m. and midnight. Remember to keep your routine consistent. An average bedtime routine could be the following:

- **7:00 p.m.:** Brush their teeth and change their diaper.
- **7:15 p.m.:** Enjoy quiet time before bedtime. (Read a book or tell a story.)
- **7:30 p.m.:** Put your baby into their crib and kiss them goodnight.

While doing the final check in your toddler's nursery, see that the environment is safe.

While this routine is ideal and convenient for most parents, you can also follow other steps if your lifestyle requires it. Following are four steps that end with your child in bed:

1. **Take a bath.** This is the time of the day to bathe your children since they may not be the cleanest after a day of playing. It is also a great time for the other partner to be involved in the bedtime routine. Sometimes a toddler switches between parents and now prefers mom or dad. Bath time for us may be lighting candles and playing some soft music, but that is not your baby's idea of a bath time. For them it should be fun, so splash around. Typically, bath time can last anywhere from five to seven minutes.

2. **Brush teeth, go potty, and put on pajamas.** This signals their brains to ready their bodies for sleep.

3. **Have play time.** Yes, play time. Go to their nursery, sit on the floor, and ask them what they want to do. I want you to play during their bedtime routine. This may surprise most parents. Normally we think of toddlers as difficult to put to bed, so why rile them up right before? Well, you and your child can have a connection time and one-on-one time with

each other. This helps them feel secure because they were able to have your full attention. The challenging part about this is that you cannot go into their bedroom with an idea of what you want to do. Sometimes you are rushed, and you want to read a certain short book and get done with it. Try not to do that. Set a timer or let them know you have X amount of time to play. Tell them it is entirely their choice, "Let's dance or let's play. You tell." You are giving your child up to 15 minutes of authority, and that is amazing for them. However, be mindful that this time has no screen time; this is purely you or your partner with your child. Get as much energy out of them as possible.

4. **Read some books.** I want you to read one or two books. They could be anything your toddler likes.

There is a reason for this bedtime routine. It is the key for a good night's sleep. Your toddler is capable of handling their sleep. You do not want you to have your toddler conditioned thinking you have to help them fall asleep. A bedtime routine is a mystical and amazing opportunity for you to invest in your child. Just remember to be consistent with the routines.

## ANSWERS TO COMMON QUESTIONS

Since the term *toddlers* cover the ages between one and three, there will be a lot of changes that you will need to make. You may have the following questions:

- Should I give my toddler a blanket or stuffed animal?
- When should I transition to a big-kid bed?
- Should I try co-sleeping with a toddler?

### *Should I Give my Toddler a Blanket or Stuffed Animal?*

Most times, a cozy blanket or a special stuffed toy can help as a sleep aid for toddlers. Everyone has specific essentials they rely on for sleep. It could be anything from the sound of a clock ticking, hugging a pillow, or leaving socks on during the night. It is normal for a toddler to wake up to ten times during the night on average, hence when their sleep conditions have changed over the course of the night, they will cry out more often. Do your toddler a favor and let them sleep with a blanket or stuffed toy if they are used to it because it gives them familiarity and comfort.

### *When Should I Transition to a Big-Kid Bed?*

It is a good idea to consider transitioning from a crib if any of the following is true for your toddler:

- They can climb out of the crib.
- Your toddler is undergoing the process of potty training.
- Your toddler does not fit in the crib.
- You have another baby on the way.

However, you may want to hang on to that crib for as long as possible. If they are happy there, leave them! The only reason to move a toddler immediately is if they are trying to jump out of the crib—making it a safety concern.

I would say two and a half years old is the earliest you should begin transitioning to a bigger bed. They are not cognitively ready for this type of responsibility before that time. If you do switch them to a bed before their time, they may not be able to resist the urge of getting out of bed and coming to find you, exploring the house, or playing games in their room. A lot of people think they can solve a sleep problem by moving to a bed since the child is not happy in the crib. However, that is not going to happen. If your toddler has sleep struggles in the crib, moving to the bed will make matters worse. Work on your issues with the child still in the crib. Once they are doing well and continue to do so for about a month, you can start the transition.

### Should I Try Co-Sleeping With my Toddler?

This is a tricky question. There are a few things that are important to consider if you choose to co-sleep with your infant. I just want to put it out there that there is no right or wrong, it is more of a parenting style choice. Co-sleeping is when you and your baby are physically sleeping closer together. With infants, co-sleeping is not recommended because of the Sudden Death Infant Syndrome (SIDS). However, as your baby grows, co-sleeping does become less dangerous. Co-sleeping with a toddler has fewer risks than doing so with an infant.

While it is a lovely feeling to be sleeping with your toddler, you also need to be on the lookout for the point at which co-sleeping has a negative impact on you or your toddler. Some parents may not get a good night's sleep. Toddlers might start associating sleep to being physically close to their parents, and it would prove to be difficult for the child to sleep if the parent is not around. As parents, we do not want to build that obstacle for our children.

When you do make the decision to end co-sleeping and move your toddler to their own space, it will provide a healthy space between you two. Sleep independence can be assisted by the following:

- Rather than sharing a bed, you could set up a crib in the same room.
- Stretch the process over time. Be patient and do not rush any change.
- Establish a positive bedtime routine. Make it fun!
- Speak to a professional. They can guide you better when you feel lost and stuck.

As a parent, I know your child's safety and happiness are extremely important to you. You want to build the safest and most comfortable environment for your child. Because sleep is such a vital element in our lives, it is a positive and healthy step to carve out independent spaces for each individual in the family.

In the western part of the world, space is emphasized. However, in other parts of the world, it is quite a different story altogether. Co-sleeping was being discussed at work, and my colleagues mentioned how in their countries (Cameroon, Nigeria, and The Philippines), co-sleeping is completely normal; in fact it begins from an early age. Oftentimes, there are parents and at least two children in one room, and all activities take place within that room. I was surprised to hear that it is a part of the norm there. Space and co-sleeping are privileges which the more affluent countries are privy to. This helped me realize how blessed Mirabelle, Mercy, Ava, and Mia are.

## REMEMBER

As you near the next age range, things will change again. Often, when you involve a 3-year-old in bedtime procedures, there is a honeymoon period, and everything goes well in the first couple of weeks. Once the novelty wears off, and the child thinks they can get out of this, play, or walk around, trouble begins. If this happens, you need to nip it in the bud. If your toddler does come to visit you suddenly on week 3, you should march them back to bed and tell them you are not allowed to get out of bed. Then, state a consequence.

When you are ready to involve your children in bedtime decisions, it is a fun time. It is a rite of passage in a way. You can get them excited about it, they can help you pick out the bedding, or a stuffed toy. That will make it fun for them. Be clear on their responsibilities and rules around bed.

# 6

# HOW PRESCHOOLERS SLEEP

Honestly, the preschooler age (3-5-years-old) is extremely adorable. They are at an age when they can talk, walk, and have conversations with you. You enjoy their curiosity and their company. Mercy was a box of entertainment, as were Ava and Mia. All of them together was a different story. Mirabelle and I would not be able to get a single word in with all their chatter.

Getting all my daughters to sleep was a feat Mirabelle and I would celebrate each day. Because Mirabelle and I divided our sleep time and responsibilities, it was manageable.

## HOW MUCH SLEEP DO THEY NEED?

At this age, sleep is important for your children to grow up healthy. On an average, children in this age bracket need around 10 to 13 hours of sleep during a 24-hour period. By this age, their nap is also cut down to one nap per day, while older children may not be napping at all.

While naps are reduced to just one a day and are eventually eliminated, preschoolers can still benefit from a good nap during the day. It is a good recharging time for your child. You can do this by setting a routine for nap times or down time which entails relaxing quiet time for your child. You will be bombarded with protests when you suggest nap time to your child in the middle of the day, so you could use the term quiet time instead. This way your child will understand over time that it is meant to be a quiet afternoon. It may even help them nod off. Keep this time to at least an hour a day.

This age can come with quite a few sleep problems. The most common is the fight against going to sleep and waking up regularly through the night. They will resist you putting them to bed because preschoolers' minds are busy and buzzing with the day's events. Most children at this age can also experience nightmares, sleepwalking, and nighttime fears.

## SHOULD YOUR PRESCHOOLER STILL BE NAPPING?

Does your preschooler still take a nap, or are those days over? We know that naps play a vital role in sustaining new learning in infants, and new research shows that naps help preschoolers learn too. Researchers from the University of Arizona studied verb learning in 3-year-old children and found that those who napped after learning new verbs had a better understanding of the words when tested 24 hours later (*Study Finds Naps May Help Preschoolers Learn*, 2017). Around 3 years is when children start napping less. So, if your preschooler is not getting a daily nap, you should not fret. Sleep experts say it is the total amount of sleep your child gets. If your child is not getting sleep at night, make sure you create an opportunity for them to nap during the day.

I want to share signs which indicate your child is ready to give up afternoon naps and signs that your child needs to keep them. This will make it easier for you to understand the next step you want to take.

When Mercy and Ava were this age, we clearly saw the signs they were ready to give their nap time up. While Mirabelle and I were upset that their nap time was up, it was also an indication our baby girls were growing up. Mercy would protest nap time and would do every-thing else other than nap. She would talk, want to play, and then end up dozing off for only 20 minutes. This became a pattern, and then we realized she was ready to let go of her afternoon nap.

When Ava entered preschool age, we thought she might give up her nap time as easily as Mercy, but we were wrong. Each child is unique. Whenever it was Ava's nap time, and we didn't put her down to nap, we would notice her yawn, and then her eyes would be droopy. There were even instances when she fell asleep in the car, and that was when we realized Ava was definitely not ready to give up her nap time.

### *Signs Your Child is Ready to Ditch the Afternoon Nap*

Just know that your child is not going to tell you they are ready to let go off their naps themselves, you will have to look out for the following signs:

- **New Bedtime Struggles:** When you notice that your child is taking longer to fall asleep at night or waking up earlier than usual in the morning, it could be an indication that the afternoon nap is throwing their entire sleep balance off. It is providing them with extra sleep they do not need; hence, the nighttime struggle to fall asleep at their usual time.

- **Protesting Nap Time:** If your child is against naps, they do not stay in bed, they keep complaining that they do not want to nap, and they do not fall asleep at all, those are clear signs that your child is done with naps.
- **A Pleasant Temperament:** When your child is in a good and stable mood during the day, even without their nap, then you will know they are good to go without. If your child retains their usual energy (apart from the normal ups and downs during the day), this suggests they do not require naps anymore.
- **Calm Mornings:** If your child is sleeping well without an afternoon nap, wakes up without your help, and is in a good mood in the morning, then they are ready to proceed to a non-napping phase in life.

### *Signs Your Child is not Ready to let go of Their Afternoon Nap*

- **Effortless Naps:** When you see that your child responds positively to naps, naps for more than an hour, and falls asleep easily without any resistance, they are not ready to give up their afternoon naps.
- **Foul mood or Behavior:** If your child is

moody, agitated, and irritable when they miss an afternoon nap, it is a sign that they are not ready to say goodbye to their nap as yet.

- **Dozing in the car:** If your child falls asleep during a short car ride, it serves as a sign that they still require their afternoon nap.
- **Sleepy:** As I have mentioned before, a child will never convey their readiness to give up their nap time. However, you will be able to tell by their body language. Things like constant yawning, going unusually quiet, less movement, and sleepy eyes mean they need their afternoon nap.
- **Lots of Energy:** This may come as a surprise, but sometimes when your child forgoes their afternoon nap, they may have a burst of hyperactivity followed by a slump. Therefore, if you observe them being fidgety or extremely hyperactive, it is another sign that they are not ready to give up their afternoon nap.

## THE PERFECT BEDTIME ROUTINE FOR YOUR PRESCHOOLER

A consistent and positive bedtime routine works wonders with putting your child to sleep. On average, most preschoolers are ready for bed by 7:30 p.m. Try the following bedtime routine:

- **7:00 p.m.:** Have your child brush their teeth, use the restroom, and change into pajamas.
- **7:15 p.m.:** Enjoy interactive playtime, book reading, cuddling with your child.
- **7:30 p.m.:** Tuck them into bed and kiss them goodnight.

Moreover, apart from their bedtime, you can incorporate a few changes throughout the day to establish a healthy and positive bedtime routine:

- Identify and answer their tired cues.
- Have consistent bedtime routines.
- Manage their nighttime needs before bedtime.
- A reward chart highlights your child's good behavior. You can put a gold star or smiley face whenever they keep up with a positive routine.

You can also educate yourself through watching YouTube tutorials on bedtime routines which suit your child and your schedule. They are more interactive and provide easy engagement. Days when I did not feel like reading or researching, I would watch YouTube tutorials. Moreover, I included my daughters in this and gave them the opportunity to see what they like and asked them what they would prefer. You can also tailor make a bedtime routine with your child to make it creative and fun!

The environment you create is also important in establishing a bedtime routine; see that it is soothing. Build an environment which feels safe, secure, comfortable, and enjoyable but also set limits. Make sure to have interactive communications with your child before they sleep. Most importantly, be patient with your child and yourself.

## TIME TO PUT THOSE PRESCHOOL BEDTIME PROBLEMS TO REST

You may think you are done with bedtime issues by this age, but you are not. Your children will still show resistance to sleep. Bedtime just means the end of the day for them, which equates to the end of fun, endless chatter, and playtime. Because I used to take turns with Mirabelle putting our daughters to sleep, I have firsthand experience. Ava, my middle child, is quite talkative and very imaginative, so her ritual before bedtime was to tell me a story rather than me telling her a story. It would start off with, "Daddy, today I want to tell you the story of the dragon and the mountain," and then by the end, she would ask me to complete it for her. As a father, these were the most precious moments with Ava.

Apart from the obvious cuteness of this experience, it was also Ava's way of prolonging the period before actual sleep. Do not underestimate your children; they are smarter than you may think! There can be a range of problems with bedtime in this age group.

### *A Frenzied Bedtime*

Most times the end of the day means you are rushing home from work, wrapping up dinner, or getting done with the day's work. Naturally, you will also be rushing to put your child to sleep. Slow down! Take a deep breath. Step back and remind yourself that you've got this! Bedtime will happen regardless, so put the stress away and channel your nervous energy into making your child's bedtime predictable, relaxing, peaceful, and regular.

I have reiterated throughout the book how important a consistent bedtime is from day one. It establishes a routine, and the routine is comfortable. First, put your chaotic energy away and then focus on your child and their bedtime routine. Make sure there is no screen time right before bed. While you are putting them to bed, tuck them in, ask them to talk to you about how their day went, share stories, and kiss them goodnight when you see them falling asleep.

### Bedtime Resistance

This is a universal problem. Believe me when I say you are not alone in this. Your child will rarely ever want to sleep when it is time. A tip I would like to share here is that it is not just the bedtime routine that matters; it is also the time leading up to the routine. Naturally, if a child is stimulated, the environment is abuzz, or the technology is on, it is hard to sleep. Even you would not want to sleep then. These are all distractions.

The aim is to have a peaceful and quiet time before starting the bedtime routine. When there is not too much noise and the environment is calm, you will notice your child slow down. They may start to feel sleepy and eventually not resist bedtime.

### Not Wanting to Sleep Alone

There will be times when your child wants you to stay in their room until they fall asleep. They need you to cuddle them, tell them nonstop stories, and need to feel your physical presence. While this is adorable, it is also not the best situation for your child's sleeping habits. As discussed before, you should look to motivating your child to sleep alone when you think they are ready. You can do this by hyping up the process, highlighting their independence, giving them a blanket or a stuffed toy, or having the night light switched on. Moreover, make the bedtime routine fun; spend some time with your child before they sleep so they do not feel alone.

If your child asks you to stay even after these tips or they call out to you, try to not go, stay, or return to their room. It sounds harsh, but you need them to build their habits. You know you have given enough time and done the bedtime routine, so your child is ready to sleep. By cutting these requests off initially, you will nip the problem of not wanting to sleep alone early on. The aim is to not have the child expecting you to sleep in their bed every night. However, be patient because these changes do not take place overnight; it is a process. Give yourself and your child the space and time to adjust.

### Waking up Frequently During the Night

If your child is waking up frequently during the night and has a hard time falling back asleep, then you can employ the same tactics you employ as mentioned above. However, if your child has a night terror or a nightmare, please be quick in responding. Talk about their dream, pacify them, comfort them, and stay with them until they fall back asleep.

### Not Staying in their Designated Bed

It is 7:30 p.m., you have put your child to sleep (or you think you have), and you leave their room. Except you hear the pitter patter of small feet behind you. You turn your head and there your child is—awake and smiling at you. There goes all your effort! Worry not. This is also common for most preschool aged children. They know they have the independence and the ability to stroll out so they will.

Either your child wants something, such as a stuffed toy or water, or they need to use the bathroom. Make sure they take care of all these things before their bedtime. More importantly, if they get up and walk out without reason, do not give them too much attention and return them to bed immediately.

### Staying up Late

By the time your child gets ready for bedtime and is ready to pass out, it is also past your bedtime now. If your child is taking longer to sleep, then you may want to look at cutting back on the duration of daytime naps.

Moreover, be mindful of the time your child is spending in bed. Sometimes it can surpass their sleep needs. You want to get the ideal sleep window for your child so either postpone your child's bedtime routine by 15 minutes to 25 minutes or move back their wake time by 15 to 25 minutes.

### Nighttime Bed Wetting

Since children at this age do not wear diapers, your child may experience bedwetting. This also increases the probability of children waking up during the night. Following is a list of reasons for bedwetting:

- Sometimes children do not wake up from a deep sleep when their bladder is full.
- Some children produce more than average urine and do not wake up to use the potty.
- Some children have a small bladder and cannot contain all the urine.
- Attention Deficit Hyperactivity Disorder (ADHD) children have a higher probability of wetting their bed.

Bedwetting is nothing to be alarmed about. It is a part of your child's emotional and physical development and will stop for most children as they grow older.

## REMEMBER

We are human, and as much as we try, we make mistakes as well. Hence, there will be days when you find yourself giving up and just letting your child have screen time before sleeping or passing out on the couch instead of their bed. When that happens, tell yourself it is okay. However, do not make it a pattern. Focus on your mood, notice your triggers, and work on them. Then, focus on your child. When you are in a better mood, it will be easier to deal with your child. Be consistent in teaching them good sleeping habits, it pays off.

# 7

# HOW SCHOOL-AGED CHILDREN SLEEP

## HOW MUCH SLEEP DO THEY NEED?

B y the time your child hits the 5-year mark, they will begin school. You will notice that their time and energy is now being divided into school time, activities, and socializing. Bedtime for this age group keeps getting pushed further and further. By 6 years, it may still be 7:30 p.m., and as their age progresses, it may extend by 30 minutes or so. Overall, the range for bedtimes could be anywhere between 7:30 p.m. to 10:00 p.m.

The average amount of sleep a child this age needs is around 9 to 13 hours, and nap times are completely cut out. By the time they turn 10-years-old, the average sleep they need per day is 10 hours. On average, children this age take around 20 minutes to fall asleep, but this does depend on how sleepy they are and their respective bedtime routines.

Personally, this was a wonderful time for Mirabelle and me. I thoroughly enjoyed this age because it is such an interactive and curious age. However, it also came with some challenges. Since there is a growing sense of independence, my little angels wanted their space but also craved time from us. Tapping into the perfect balance was not always possible, but we worked with what we thought was best for all of us.

## WHAT TO EXPECT?

According to the guidelines, not getting enough sleep is common in this age group. This is due to the fact that there is an increase of activities in the child's life—homework, school, extracurricular activities, and so on. Moreover, you may also see sleep problems such as teeth grinding, sleepwalking, nightmares, and noisy breathing in this age group. Sleep deprivation in this age group can affect:

- **Mood:** You will notice your child being sulky, irritable, and bad tempered. They will get annoyed easily.
- **Behavior:** They will more than likely have behavior problems, such as defiance and hyperactivity.
- **Cognitive Ability:** They will be inattentive, have foggy memory, slower reaction time, and hampered creativity. All which are imperative for studying in school.
- **Lifestyle:** They will have a hard time waking up and be lazier and more lethargic.

## COMMON SLEEP ISSUES AND SOLUTIONS

Sleep is the strongest habit-forming behavior we have. If a child learned early on to sleep with somebody or to rely on an external prop, this problem can linger. While you may have hoped they would outgrow this, as many as 85% of babies who struggle to sleep well turn into toddlers and school aged children who don't sleep well. It comes down to the relationships we form with sleep. Hence, it is imperative to create a schedule and sleep routine from the beginning. Luckily this can be fixed by learning new habits and breaking old habits. Around 20-30% of children have sleep problems.

### Disruptive Sleep Apnea

Sleep apnea disrupts a child's breathing, and sometimes they even stop breathing while sleeping. The signs of sleep apnea are snoring, struggling to breathe during the night, and daytime fatigue. Do consult a doctor if you feel your child has sleep apnea.

### Night Terrors and Nightmares

Agitation during deep sleep could be a sign of night terrors. They occur during the first hour after falling asleep. However, they are not as common as nightmares and fade out by puberty. While your child may not remember the content of the night terror, it can be scary for the observer—you. On the other hand, nightmares are common in school-age children and do have the ability to wake children up from sleep. As they grow up, children realize dreams are nothing but dreams. Nightmares occur during the second half of the night.

### Sleep Talking and Sleepwalking

Sleep talking is nothing to worry about. It occurs when children are excited or anxious about a certain event. You can talk to your child about whatever is on their mind which will alleviate their concerns.

Sleepwalking is a phenomenon during which your child's body is awake, but their mind is asleep. It could be genetic or due to anxiety in the child. However, it does not require treatment and children grow out of it. Both sleep talking and sleepwalking occur during the first hour of falling asleep.

### Teeth-Grinding and Thumb-Sucking

Grinding teeth is common and is not a cause of alarm. However, if your child is still thumb-sucking after at five, it could be damaging to their teeth.

### Needing to Sleep With a Parent

From 3 to 10 years, children think they need a parent present. It is a habit. You can break it by gradually teaching them to fall asleep independently. Wean yourself out of the bed and out of the room. Moreover, older children can be educated. Get your child on board and make it a fun process for them. Believe me, learned sleep skills last for a lifetime. Practice the following tips to help your child overcome their sleep issues:

- Reduce screen time 2-3 hours before bedtime. This includes TV, video games, and phones.
- Get in some physical activity during the day.

- A light snack is okay before bedtime, but avoid heavy meals.
- The sleeping environment should be dark and quiet.
- Research behavioral approaches.
- Soak in the natural sunlight each day.
- Stay clear from caffeinated drinks.

Remember, everything does not happen overnight. And as I always say, be patient with the process!

# 8

# SLEEP TRAINING

When Mercy was born, I thought I had everything nailed. As a father, I wanted to be more proactive and involved in the entire process and journey. However, all of my reading and research was not the same as living through the experience. There were days when Mirabelle would have to remind me to take it slow and easy because I felt I needed to have everything on point.

When it came to sleep training Mercy, Mirabelle and I tried our best to create the perfect routine for her. There was a lot of back and forth, failed attempts, anger, moods, and impatience, but it paid off. Moreover, when Ava and Mia were born, we had so much more firsthand knowledge about sleep training the we were less anxious. Before sleep training your child using any method, you need to pay close attention to their bedtime routine and habits.

## WHAT DOES SLEEP TRAINING LOOK LIKE?

What exactly is the goal of sleep training? We need our child to sleep undisturbed for a few hours through the night, and if they do wake up, we need them to self-soothe and settle themselves to fall back asleep. There are various methods that can be used to train your child. You just have to find one that works well with your child's temperament and your lifestyle.

When your child is sleep trained, they are able to sleep 9 to 12 hours through the night which results in a well-rested child. This also has a positive impact on their behavior. Sleep training takes a few days to a week to help your child sleep; however, the key is to remain constant and patient. As Confucius said, "It does not matter how slowly you go as long as you do not stop." While the best time to start sleep training is usually between 4 to 6 months, you can still sleep train with older children as well. All hope is not lost, and it is never too late.

## THE METHODS

It is the 21st century, and it is easy to Google and research methods and techniques for sleep training. However, I have compiled everything I know, along with my experiences in one place to make it time-friendly and convenient for you. Because believe me, time and convenience are luxuries as parents. While there are numerous established methods for sleep training, you can also devise your own if none seem to be working out for you.

Mirabelle and I used different methods for all three of our daughters. This was not because we wanted to experiment with each method, rather our daughters have different temperaments and different methods suited all three. While we were lucky with Mercy and Mia, we were not that lucky with Ava. However, with time and patience, I believe Mirabelle and I did a great job at sleep training our little angels.

### *Cry it Out Method*

The crying it out method or controlled comforting method sounds a bit cold and harsh. While most parents do not opt for this method, you will find that some do, and it works for them. If you try it, remember all babies are not the same. Let's be honest, we are humans. If you have sleep struggles and get to a tipping point where you think nothing else works, you may end up resorting to this method. However, it is not the healthiest method for all babies.

Statistically this method has proven to work for a lot of parents but not for everyone. Temperament plays a huge part in this. You have to look at why it works. In essence, you are giving your baby a consistent answer to a question. That question being, "Are you going to help me sleep?" Your answer with this method is always, "You will work it out on your own, and I will be back in the morning."

To sleep train your baby using the cry it out method, you can do the following:

- Make sure you have a consistent and calming bedtime routine.
- Observe your baby for signs of weariness.
- Snuggle and cuddle your baby and say goodnight.
- Place your baby in the crib.
- Talk to your baby until they are quiet and then leave the room.

If crying it out will work, it will happen in 3 to 5 days, and the crying should become less and less. If the crying is not lessening, then you need to step back and re-examine. Catch a breath and rethink if this is right for the temperament of your child.

I understand how easy it sounds as a method. If you could be done in 3 days with sleep training, it would be wonderful, but it may not be the ideal situation. While I personally find this method slightly traumatic for babies, one of my colleagues said this was the only method he practiced with his baby, and it worked miraculously. Ahmed, my colleague from Pakistan, mentioned how the cry it out method worked for his children. This was something his mother-in-law had said they practiced with their children, and it always worked.

As opposed as I was, I tried to convince Mirabelle to try this method with Ava for a couple of days to see if it would work out. Ava had a cranky disposition as a baby, so we decided to give it a shot. However, on the second night, we could not go through with it because we just could not muster up the strength to stay away from her while she cried. We then decided to try the camping method, also known as the chair method.

### Parental Presence Method

Parental presence, simply put is using your presence to help your baby self-settle. While this method is effective, it does take longer to instill. It requires parents to put in more effort since they will have to stay in their baby's room for at least a week to 10 days whenever their baby is awake. This reinforces the baby's belief that the parents are around. However, you cannot interact much with your baby since the aim of this method is to reduce and break the link between your attention and your baby's sleep behavior. Following are some ways you can use parental presence as a method to sleep train your baby:

- Decide a bedtime.
- Establish a positive and healthy bedtime routine.
- Place your baby in their crib. Try doing this while they are drowsy, nearly asleep, or awake.
- Pat your baby in a gentle manner and wish them goodnight.
- Lie down on a bed or chair in your baby's nursery, switch on a night light, and pretend to fall asleep in a place where your baby can see you clearly.
- If your baby does wake up during the night and seems distraught, make a soft noise or movement so your baby knows you are still in the room.
- If your baby does get extremely distraught,

sooth them with words or gentle touches. Try not to pick them in your arms.

- Give yourself and your baby a couple of minutes before pretending to fall asleep in their room again.
- Continue this cycle every time your baby awakens and seems distressed. Repeat this pattern for daytime naps as well.
- You will have to continue this cycle for seven nights.
- After the first three nights, you can return to your room. However, keep in mind that there has to be minimal sleep disturbance for you to return to your room.
- If you find that your baby's sleep is becoming disturbed again, you can begin this cycle all over.

We tried this method with Mia because she had difficulty sleeping when we were not around. We did try the fading method with her at first, but her sleep association did not fade with time, and she would end up crying every time we put her down. Hence, we decided to switch to this method, and luckily, it worked. Mia took a while to self-settle, but she eventually did. Mirabelle and I would take turns staying in Mia's room. On average, it takes seven nights, but because Mia was slightly more dependent on our presence, it took around 11 days. In the end, our patience and time paid off.

### Camping out/Chair Method

Another method to train your baby is the camping out or chair method. It is pretty similar to parental presence. While this method allows you to not sleep in your baby's room, it restricts you from leaving your baby while they are crying for even a few minutes. This strategy can take up to three weeks in helping your baby sleep by themselves. If you opt for this method to train your baby, it is advisable to plan ahead and be patient with the process between each step. To make it easier on yourself and your baby:

- Pick a suitable bedtime.
- Establish a healthy bedtime routine.
- Place your baby in their crib when they are tired as opposed to when they are already asleep.

Just as parental presence had steps, so does camping out. Try your best to follow these steps in order and remember to be patient with yourself and your baby. All of us take time to learn and adjust. Each step of the camping out method may take up to two to three nights. Before you progress to the next step, make sure your baby is comfortable. These are the steps:

1. Sit next to your baby and pat them gently until they fall asleep. Leave the room once they have fallen asleep.
2. Put a chair next to the crib and sit next to your baby but do not pat them. Let your baby fall asleep before leaving the room.
3. Place a chair further from the crib and let your baby fall asleep before leaving the room.
4. Finally, place the chair just outside the bedroom door.

If your baby does wake up, begin to repeat the steps you used at bedtime.

We ended up trying this method for Ava. For the first week, Mirabelle camped out with Ava, and for the remaining two weeks, I did. Mirabelle and I would sing lullabies to Ava to calm and soothe her. Ava did cry during the process, but she adjusted, and finally we managed to sleep train her. It worked wonders for us. We went from taking an hour to put Ava to bed, to taking five to seven minutes to put her to sleep.

### *Fading Method*

This method involves very few or no tears at all. As the name suggests, it means to eventually fade out your child's bedtime routine. For instance, if you have been using a certain method to put your child to sleep such as patting, rocking, or singing, you will lessen the amount of time you employ that method over a period of time until you finally stop. We can rock or sing our child to sleep; however, we do not want them to be entirely dependent on us to do the same each time they have to fall asleep.

For instance, imagine that your baby is used to movement before sleeping, and they need it to fall asleep. Rather than going cold turkey and saying no to all types of movement, nursing, and holding, what if you just slowly reduce the time spent on that movement? If you continue to stretch your baby in their tolerance of no movement, your baby will be able to fall asleep without movement altogether eventually.

The pace is up to you, and it is flexible. If you are a stickler for rules, this might not be the method for you. This method is effective because rather than jumping straight into a sleep method which requires rules, you can gently wean your child of sleep associations without the shock. (No cold turkey.)

You can begin to use this method when your child is four months old. The duration of the method solely depends on your consistency, your child's temperament, and your pace. It can, on average, take anywhere between three weeks to three months. So, while it is a less traumatic method and guarantees very few tears, it is not the fastest.

We tried this method with Mercy when we began to sleep train her. Mirabelle and I had decided it was the least traumatic one for us and for Mercy. Being new parents, dealing with tears was overwhelming for us. Initially, Mirabelle and I used to take turns with Mercy, we would rock her to sleep in the first few months, and she would sleep easily. She was not a fussy baby by nature, so this method was perfect for her. This was also our first time trying sleep training methods, and we were hesitant and wondered if the first method would even work! Luckily for us, it did. Mercy took to it like fish to water. However, it took us around a month to complete. So if you have time on your hands and are patient, I suggest you opt for the fading method. Because I was equally active as Mirabelle, it was easier to alternate turns rather than one partner getting burnt out.

### The "Happiest Baby" Method

Harvey Karp is a pediatrician who invented the "Happiest Baby Method." He outlines the five S's in his method which aim to recreate the environment the child had in the mother's womb to help them sleep. The five S's are:

1. **Swaddle:** Swaddling is the act of wrapping your baby in a thin blanket. Make sure their arms are inside the blanket. This wrapping recreates the feeling of being in the womb, and it helps your baby from flailing their arms and crying. It is also a cue for your baby to sleep. Do swaddle your baby for each sleep time and use a thin blanket rather than a warmer one. The tip for the perfect swaddle is to wrap your baby tight enough so that they cannot wiggle out, but you must leave enough room in order for them to bend their legs. Do not swaddle your baby when they are awake. You can wean your baby off of swaddling after four to five months.

2. **Side or Stomach Position:** The next step after swaddling is to lay them on their side or stomach—only to soothe them. This is not for sleeping since it could increase the risk of sudden infant death syndrome (SIDS). When

your baby is crying, hold them in a side or tummy down position. Once they have fallen asleep, lay your child on their back.

3. **Shush:** Shushing is comforting and calming, helps to stop your baby crying, and helps put them to sleep. Contrary to popular belief, newborns do not need peace and quiet since the womb is quite loud. They sleep better in a noisier environment. You can say "sshh" loudly into your baby's ear while jiggling them. This sound will calm them.

4. **Swing:** Swinging is essentially jiggling with tiny quick movements. This is a comforting motion for your baby when they are upset and crying. Do this while your baby is swaddled, held sideways in your arms, and you are shushing them. Remember to keep their head supported and to jiggle softly, not shake them.

5. **Suck:** Sucking is giving your baby a pacifier or their thumb to suck on when they are upset or crying since it provides comfort and relaxation to them. Pacifiers lessen the chance of SIDs; hence, babies can keep it in bed.

Apply the five S's together in order to have your baby happy and sleepy in your arms.

By now, you understand how a baby's sleep patterns change, how to keep up with them, and how to start sleep training them according to your chosen method. Know that there will be bumps along the way, but do not let that deter you. Once again, be mindful of the time it takes to learn new things and be patient with the process. Choose a method which suits your parenting style and your lifestyle.

## TROUBLESHOOTING

You may think you have everything going just the way it should be and according to the manuals. However, you are still not seeing the result of your hard work. You are trying everything, yet your child is not responding well to your sleep training methods. What could it be? It could be due to many things:

- You are sleeping in your child's room.
- There are blurry boundary lines and no limits.
- There is a lack of routine.
- Bedtimes do not remain constant.
- The build-up to bedtime is shaky.
- They are experiencing extinction bursts. (This is a behavioral term which explains that an unwanted behavior gets worse before it

improves when you are trying to get free of it. It occurs commonly in the "cry it out" sleep training method.)
- You are feeding your child through the night.
- You are transitioning from the crib to a toddler bed too soon.

Moreover, you will also need to pay attention to the details that do matter when it comes to sleep training. One of the key factors is the environment and sleeping conditions of where your child sleeps. I would suggest you set up your child's room as a calm and peaceful space. You can keep the following factors in mind when planning your child's room or nursery:

- Buy a comfortable and high-quality mattress.
- Keep distractions at a minimum in the room.
- Have a ceiling fan installed.
- Install a speaker.
- Buy a nightlight.
- Find the right temperature.
- Add good quality black out blinds.
- Paint the room a tranquil color such as light blue or light green. These colors are known to be calming.

Establishing a healthy and positive bedtime routine (as I have covered in previous chapters) can do wonders for sleep training your child. There will be ups and downs, no matter how hard you are working, but it will be okay. Parenting is all about patience and going with the flow.

# 9

# FOR THE CHILD WITH SPECIAL NEEDS

Having a child with special needs will require more care and time from you. Around 80% of children with developmental incapacities suffer from sleep issues. This will influence the quality of their sleep. Your child may have reflux, sensory issues, or seizures which can hamper their ability to sleep.

Moreover, if your child has autism or sensory processing disorder (SPD), sleep will have a totally different meaning for you. Your child may not sleep well, or they may get up during odd hours at night, which will also equate to you not sleeping and not being able to recharge. Other issues do come into play such as sensitivities or insensitiveness to light and noise and repeated breakdowns. The lack of sleep only makes these issues more challenging.

SPD means your child will have difficulty managing any information gathered by their senses. Hence, their brain will have trouble responding to this type of sensory material. Children with autism have disturbances in their social and emotional brain correspondence, and they may have trouble with sound processing.

## TIPS FOR SUCCESSFUL SLEEP TRAINING

I want to share tips with you which will be helpful in sleep training your child with special needs.

- Establish a routine.
- Decrease screen time.
- Do not give your child food or water at least two hours before bedtime.
- Be consistent and stable.
- View your child's sleep issues as a habit.

### *Routine*

While a routine is healthy and important for all children, if your child has special needs, then a routine is absolutely vital. If your child has autism, SPD, or ADHD, they will be calmer and feel more confident when they know what the next day entails. This applies to daily activities as well as sleep. You will need to pay attention to creating and following a consistent pattern of nap time, sleep time, and wake up time. Their brain will start associating a healthy routine with this schedule and they will take it as a cue.

### Screen Time

The blue light that is emitted from screens affects our sleep since it hampers the production of melatonin in our brain. Children with special needs sometimes end up using devices and screens for longer periods of time, which stimulates their brain and pushes it into overdrive. This is not healthy for them or their melatonin production. I would advise you to cut their screen time down in general but also regulate screen time before bedtime. Have them put their devices down at least an hour before their established bedtime.

### Food & Water Before Bed

Children with special needs often have a sensitive digestive system. If your child has reflux, then do not feed them at least two hours before bedtime. Make sure dinner is not made from ingredients which can cause reflux such as dairy, gluten, spices, and sugar.

### Consistency

For children with special needs, everything needs to be clear. Once you have decided on something, it has to remain that way. For instance, if you have decided 7:00 p.m. as bedtime, then you must stick to it consistently. This is one of the key factors in improving sleep. Furthermore, you need to clearly communicate what you expect of them and be clear about what will happen next. This way, they will understand more easily.

### *Habits*

As adults, we get accustomed to our lifestyle and the habits we form. The same goes for your child. You need to provide them with the same items to use every night while they sleep such as their blanket, a stuffed toy, and the same pillow. Your child will begin to make associations with these objects, take them as a cue, and find comfort in them. Help them associate their room with a place to sleep, not play. Use sleep props such as a pillow, blanket, or toy and then slowly start working toward letting your child sleep alone. However, if your child is prone to seizures, you will need to set up a camera in their room to monitor them during the night.

Remember that children with special needs require the same amount of sleep as children without special needs. While it may be difficult sometimes, know that you are doing a good enough job, and you will be able to work through the hiccups.

# 10

# FOR MULTIPLES

M irabelle and I do not have twins, as you must know by now. However, we can imagine what it must feel like in terms of raising and sleep training twins. While it is a challenge, it is possible to do with help, the right tips, and techniques.

Some of our friends have adorable twins, and we asked them for their input and help to write this chapter. While their journey was tiring and not the easiest, it was manageable with both of them helping out. They had a strong support system and learned a lot of lessons along the way.

Felix and Diane have twins. When I asked them to share their experience and tips, they said it was during the most challenging times that we bonded the most as a family. They began sleep training their twin daughters when they were four months old. They began experimenting with different methods and techniques such as the cry it out, timed checks, dream feeds, the shuffle, and dramatic wakeups.

One of the most challenging aspects about this entire phase was being able to get them on the same sleep schedule and giving them the same amount of attention. With twins, it is double the work at the same time. While it will be overwhelming, remind yourself you can get through it. It took a while for Felix and Diane. A lot of exhaustion, sleepless nights, and dedication went into getting their twins to sleep through the night.

While they initially tried the easier way of feeding the twins till they fell asleep and putting them down for the night, it was not the most effective sleep training method long-term. Diane said she would rush to her twins' cribs in their room as soon as they cried, feed them, and put them to sleep, but she knew it was time to cut the cord and teach them how to self-settle and sleep on their own. Over time, as Diane and Felix became completely sleep deprived and exhausted, they realized they had to do something.

## THE TRAINING

Like us, Diane and Felix were against the cry it out method until they ran out of patience and tried it out of desperation. It did not work out well for them. They said their twins just cried rather than sleeping. They eventually sought help from a sleep consultant who told them to look into their bodies' physiological needs and help the twins unlearn the habits they had already taught them.

The first tip she gave them was to not have the twins sleep in their (Diane and Felix's) bed. They had to have a separate room. Through sleep training, they managed to learn a lot about their twins and what their needs were. By focusing on their needs, Diane and Felix began to understand their twins much better. They said it was hard work, but by the time they were seven months old, the twins were on good sleep schedules and sleeping through the night. Following are the techniques they employed:

- Divide the work. Diane sleep trained one twin while Felix sleep trained the other twin, and they would alternate each night. It was a clear and fair division of duties.
- Put them in bed awake not asleep. The trick is that your baby needs to know they are in bed,

physically and emotionally. They will start to associate their bed with sleeping cues. Put your twins to sleep while they are awake. If you put them to sleep in their crib when they are already asleep, they will get scared when they wake up during the night. They remember being awake in their parent's arms and then waking up in a different place. Use dream feeding. Diane would feed her twins while they were asleep, and then she began to decrease the amount of feed over each night. Eventually, they began to pull back the feeding hours until it became unnecessary.

- Try different methods. Diane and Felix switched between two methods if the twins woke up during the night—shuffle method or timed checks. Yet again, this depends on your babies' dispositions. When they tried the shuffle technique, which is somewhat similar to the chair method with shushing, it did not work too well on the twins because the shushing irritated them. So, they moved to timed checks. Timed checks revolve around attending to your child as soon as they cry, comforting them by rubbing their back, shushing them, and retreating from the room. You then go back to the room and do the same actions one minute later, three minutes later, five minutes later, and then 10 minutes later, until your baby stops crying.

- Reduce their feedings. Diane and Felix would feed their twins if they woke up between 4:00 a.m. and 5:00 a.m. They slowly reduced the amount of feeding time after every second day. This allows your twins to get used to sleeping longer and out of the habit of waking for early morning feedings.
- Have a dramatic wake up. When the twins would wake up at 6:00 a.m. or would not fall asleep after being fed, they would leave the room and count to 10. Then, they re-entered the room, switched the lights on, and cheerily said good morning. This would help the twins comprehend that it was morning time and they were being taken out of bed.

Moreover, Diane and Felix were very thorough with their twins' sleep training. They recorded everything from how much they ate, the time they ate, nap times, night sleep times, when they awoke, and their responses. By doing this, they got a fair idea of how their children functioned. They also gave this record to their sleep consultant who provided feedback. It took them around four weeks to train their twins. They say the first night everyone slept through the night, they celebrated and hadn't been happier.

## RE-TRAINING

However, as babies grow, sleep regressions happen. The twins started to wake up partially and cry. Felix's response would be to bring them back to bed with him. This turned into the twins forcing themselves to wake up just so they could get into their parents' bed. Cheeky! Eventually, Diane and Felix had moved the twins back into their room. While they did enjoy the cuddles and fun time, it was not practical. Hence, they had to retrain the twins. They employed the following steps to retrain:

1. Conduct strict time checks.
2. Attend to them.
3. Do not pick them up.
4. Comfort them at the 1-, 3-, 5-, and 10-minute intervals.

It took them around three days to retrain their twins, but they had to be stricter with themselves as well. Timing is key. Diane and Felix shared their intense feelings and emotions with us on this journey of theirs. They said to be sure and focus on the feelings of it all.

These are things they had to say about the stages of the re-training process:

- It will start off with determination. You will be excited about it, and this is the time to get the sleep log ready, the duties divided, and energies up!
- You will then get to the point of disbelief over why your sleep training methods are not working. You will sometimes wonder what the point is?
- From disbelief, you will move on to the phase where you will feel you have no power or control over the situation at all.
- Then, you will begin to panic and wonder what you should do. What if I can never succeed at sleep training with not one, but two babies?
- From this stage, you will move on to the point of focus. You will remind yourself that your focus is their needs, their sleep, and their health. So, you will put aside your fears for now and spend time and effort on your twins.
- Finally, you will taste the pure joy of victory, which comes in big and small doses. When you see them sleeping peacefully at a stretch, give yourself a pat on the back.

Know that this struggle is not only true for the parents of twins but for all parents. Being a parent is not easy. We are tired, moody, irritable, and busy, yet we want to give it our best for our children. While you will want to give up sleep training and forego the idea of self-settling, know that the long-term goal you are working for is much healthier for you and your baby. While Diane and Felix are happy to share their successful advice, following it is up to you.

# 11

# WHEN NOTHING WORKS

You've tried every sleeping method, yet nothing seems to be working for you? Do not worry! You are not the problem and neither is your baby. It could very well be the method causing the issue. It could also be your child's temperament and undiagnosed sleep disorders. I just want to make you aware that all sleeping methods can fail if it's not suited to your child's temperament. Do not take it personally; it is not a reflection of your effort.

## SLEEP PERSONALITIES

Your child's lack of sleep could be due to sleep disorders, your child's temperament, or the wrong method. First, you must know your child's sleep personality.

There are two types of sleep personalities: self-soothers (babies who fall back asleep by themselves) and signalers (babies who have the tendency to cry out during the night). Most babies fall somewhere in between the two extreme ends of the spectrum.

People tend to label these traits. For instance, self-soothers are seen as "good sleepers," while signalers are "problem sleepers." However, there isn't a strict hierarchy. According to Dr. Elizabeth Super, "babies aren't good or bad sleepers," she says, "they're just different." Many heavy-lidded new parents are relieved to learn that if their baby does not sleep well, it's not something they are doing wrong. The reality is that babies are simply prone to a particular sleep mode. You can probably guess which temperament your baby has.

It's natural for all babies to wake up five to seven times per night. Although the waking periods are often undetectable for us, this cycle continues into adulthood. Babies who are self-soothers can go to sleep more easily when bedtime begins and go back to sleep on their own when they wake. Self-soothers may also stay asleep for longer periods of time or sleep through the night sooner than other babies.

If you have a self-soothing child, you may hear them wake up (perhaps babbling to themselves) and then drift off back to sleep. As a part of their soothing routine, they might use a pacifier, suck their thumb, cuddle up with a favorite blanket, or hum to themselves. Unlike self-soothers, signalers usually take longer to learn settling skills. These infants may have more difficulty falling and staying asleep, and when they wake up during the night, they may cry or call out for attention.

If your baby wakes up regularly during the night, or if they stop crying and light up when they see you enter the room, you most likely have a signaler. Learning a new sleep routine or being able to settle back into their normal routine after a holiday, illness, or developmental milestones may take longer as they discover and form self-soothing skills.

Whatever their innate sleep temperament, a child's sleep skills are a learned behavior. Nearly all children will begin to adapt and fall asleep on their own as they grow up, regardless of their sleep temperament. It may seem like self-soothers catch on more quickly, but do not worry; signalers will get there in their own time. As children develop, sleep challenges come and go, and even the calmest self-soother may have difficult phases of sleep development. Whatever your infant's sleep temperament may be, supporting great sleep habits will help them build the skills that they need for a good night's rest.

SLEEP DISORDERS

According to the American Academy of Family Physi-
cians, around 50% of children experience sleep disorders in their life. The most common sleep disorders
according to them are:

- Obstructive Sleep Apnea (1 to 5%)
- Sleepwalking (17%)
- Confusional arousals (17.3% in kids up to age
  13 and 2.9 to 4.2% in adolescents older than
  age 15)
- Sleep Terrors (1 to 6.5%)
- Nightmares (10 to 50% in 3- to 5-year-olds)
- Behavioral Insomnia (10 to 30%)
- Delayed Sleep Phase Disorder (7 to 16% in
  adolescents, specifically)
- Restless Leg Syndrome (2%)

While children do take time to sleep and will put up
resistance, if you notice them doing it more often and
not responding well to sleep training methods, it could
be the sign of a sleep disorder. The signs that your child
could have sleep disorder are:

- Your child lays awake in bed, calling out to you for another book, song, drink, or another trip to the bathroom for hours on end.
- Your child sleeps continuously for about 90 minutes in a stretch, even during the night.
- Your child scratches their legs through the night.
- Your child snores at night.

There are several sleep disorders that affect children.

### Childhood Insomnia

This is a very common disorder. Children with this disorder will find it hard to fall asleep, stay asleep, go back to sleep, or wake up. Upon waking, they will still feel sleepy. It usually leads to children being drained which affects energy levels during the day.

### Delayed Sleep Phase Syndrome

As the term suggests, this syndrome affects the child's ability to sleep on time. They will find it difficult to fall asleep at their requisite time. This pushes bedtime and wake up time later in the day. Their body clock shifts which leads to exhaustion.

## *Hypersomnia*

Children with hypersomnia will feel sleepy even after getting 7 hours of sleep. They will want to sleep even though they do not need to, which leads to daytime sleepiness. Some may even have sleep attacks where they can feel an overwhelming feeling of sleepiness during daily activities.

## *Parasomnias*

Parasomnia is an incomplete arousal between sleep stages. These disorders are mostly motor based actions; however, sometimes they can be behavioral as well. When we sleep, we go into different stages. Parasomnias can occur in non-REM and REM stages, though they commonly occur during the non-REM stage. They show up in the form of confusional arousals, night terrors, sleep walking, and very rarely sleep related eating disorders.

During confusional arousal, children sit up and look confused. They might cry, mumble, or look scared. However, they are fast asleep and do not respond. They do not have any memory of the previous night the next morning. It occurs during the first hour and a half after the onset of sleep.

Night terrors are when children sit up and scream, cry, or yell in a shrill voice. This can be scary for the parent.

Other behavioral aspects you will notice are rapid breathing, rapid heartbeat, and sweating. They are not awake during this and do not respond if spoken to. This also occurs after the first hour and a half of sleep. There is no recollection of the event the next morning.

### Obstructive Sleep Apnea

During sleep apnea, children stop breathing for around 10 seconds. Children with sleep apnea snore, sleep with open mouths, and are sleepy during the day. This can lead to irritability and, in extreme cases, heart issues.

### Behavioral and Mental Health Disorders

Refer to chapter 9.

## WHEN TO CONSULT A DOCTOR

For many parents, it is hard to know whether a child is just restless or is going through a sleep disorder. If your child has no memory of any incident during the night such as nightmares, sleep walking, or night terrors, then the chances are that your child might need medical attention. You should consider talking to a healthcare professional or seeking medical attention. It's important to have a discussion with a medical practitioner about these events especially if attempts to improve sleep have not been successful.

A doctor or a sleep specialist can provide comprehensive information and guidance on helping your child's sleep patterns and resolving sleep disorders. You should feel comfortable seeking help from medical practitioners any time concerns arise about your child. In the case that your child is going through unresolved sleep disorders, your pediatrician or a medical sleep specialist can do the following to help:

- They will help in creating a comprehensive plan to improve your child's sleep that can be followed at home.
- They may find other root causes and refer you to other specialists who might be able to help such as an ear, nose, and throat doctor or an allergist.
- They might diagnose underlying medical issues that prevent sleep such as obstructive sleep apnea.

Involving and engaging with a pediatrician or a sleep specialist can be the next step to improved sleep for your child.

# 12

# STAY IN THE LOOP

Congratulations! You have made it so far—hopefully without falling asleep due to exhaustion. By now, you have read about the importance of sleep and how to sleep train your child. I have made it clear that this process will not be easy. There will be ups and downs, but you will be able to do it!

As a father to three angles, I have gone through my fair share of experiences and lessons. Not only did I promise Mirabelle the support of being a consistent caregiver and helpful partner, but I made a promise to myself as well—to do the best I can and know that it is good enough.

When Mirabelle and I began sleep training Mercy (our first experience of sleep training), it was confusing, overwhelming, frustrating, and rewarding. There would be days when we would ponder over whether we should switch to another method or stick to the same one. But our persistence, consistency, and support of each other helped us keep our head in the game. When I felt out of sorts, Mirabelle would pull me up and shake sense into me. And I did the same for her.

There were days when I would go to work like a zombie on three hours of sleep. There were days when I would zone out while somebody would speak to me, days when exercising was not an option, and days when not seeing anyone other than Mirabelle and Mercy was the norm.

When Ava and Mia were born, we thought we were ready. We knew what sleep training method to apply, and we hoped and wished it would all work out with time. However, as Eleanor Roosevelt said, "It takes as much energy to wish as it does to plan." Hence, Mirabelle and I began planning and sleep training Ava and Mia from the time they were ready. I learned the following lessons, which I want to share with you.

- Be patient with yourself.
- Support your partner.
- Trust the process.
- Every day is a new day to start over.

- Laugh over the mistakes.
- Learn from your mistakes.
- Be consistent.
- Remember, you're in this together with your partner.
- Follow through.
- Have faith.

On the days I thought I'd had enough, I would think about these pointers, and they would make me feel much better. I hope this helps you on your journey as well!

Remember, parents play an important role in fixing their child's sleep disorders and improving their quality of sleep. There are many simple fixes and actions that can be taken by the parents to improve sleep. To summarize what we have gone through, there are many different ways for parents to help a child get the rest they need, such as:

- Encourage relaxation. Nightly rituals before bedtime can be helpful for a child to get better sleep. Parents can consider giving a warm bath or some quiet reading every night before bed. Create a comfortable environment for your child by keeping the bedroom lights dim while the child is preparing for bed. Also ensure that the room is dark and cool at night.

- Set a routine. Following the same routine every night before bedtime helps children sleep better because the child gets used to a sleep routine and pattern. Night routines can include singing a lullaby for infants or reading a book for older children. Leaving simple instructions for children to follow also helps.
- Underline the need for time together. Parents should spend time with their child before bedtime. This could include a few minutes before bed where you can talk to the child or cuddle with them and have a meaningful conversation about their day. This will give your child comfort and make them feel less restless before bed.
- Unplug electronics. Parents should not allow their child to use any electronics before bedtime. The idea is to make the bedroom an electronics-free zone at least one hour before bedtime and then start the night routine.

Remember to make positive associations with your child's bedtime rather than scolding them for not going to bed or staying up later than usual. Following is a checklist which you can go through in order to have everything in order and to help you plan:

- Establish a bedtime routine that works for your child.
- Make reward charts with your child.
- Figure out which sleeping method works best for your child.
- Create a sleep friendly environment in your room and your child's room.
- Create a consistent pattern with your child.
- Be patient with the process.

Now it is time for you to put my words into action and see the results. I want to bid you farewell with one of my favorite quotes from Confucius. "It does not matter how slowly you go, as long as you don't stop." It does not have to be a race with time or be perfect; it only has to be good enough for you and your baby!

# REFERENCES

*Cdc - how much sleep do I need? - Sleep and sleep disorders.* (2019, March 5). https://www.cdc.gov/sleep/about_sleep/how_much_sleep.html

McQuillan, M. E., Bates, J. E., Staples, A. D., & Deater Deckard, K. (2019). Maternal stress, sleep, and parenting. *Journal of Family Psychology : JFP : Journal of the Division of Family Psychology of the American Psychological Association (Division 43), 33*(3), 349–359. https://doi.org/10.1037/fam0000516

*Power napping for productivity, stress relief and health.* (n.d.). Verywell Mind. https://www.verywellmind.com/power-napping-health-benefits-and-tips-stress-3144702

*Study finds naps may help preschoolers learn.* (2017, January 30). University of Arizona News. https://news.arizona.edu/story/study-finds-naps-may-help-preschoolers-learn

# QUICK NOTE

Positive reviews from awesome customers like you help others to feel confident about choosing this book too. Could you take 60 seconds on Amazon or any platform where you got the book and share your happy experiences? There are other awesome books like *The First Time Father, The First Time Father: Baby's First Year, Sleep Training like a Pro, Single Dad Parenting like a Pro, Potty Training Like a Pro, Discipline Like a Pro, All Fathers Memorable Jokes* and others still to come. Any ideas you would like Alfie Thomas to write about or improve on, his email is always open. You can reach out to

books@alfie-thomas.com,

and https://thealfiethomas.com/

https://mirabellen.activehosted.com/f/1,

https://www.facebook.com/
groups/1253933881690907,

and https://www.instagram.com/alfiethomas.official/

We will be forever grateful. Thank you in advance for helping us out.

 SCAN ME

www.ingramcontent.com/pod-product-compliance
Lightning Source LLC
Chambersburg PA
CBHW051625120626

46551CB00014B/1946

* 9 7 8 1 9 9 8 0 8 3 0 1 5 *